UNLEASH YOUR BUSINESS MOJO!

"This book will develop your entrepreneurial mind set and get you through the first steps of starting and running your own business"

MO OBADINA FCCA, ACA

Unleash Your Business MOJO!

First published in Great Britain in 2016 by
Mo's Mojo Media (UK)
www.mosmojo.com

ISBN:
978-0-9955489-0-9

A CIP catalogue record for this book is available from the
British Library

Book design by Mo's MOJO Media (UK)

Dedication

This book is dedicated to the memory of my loving brother Femi Obadina whose light shone on everyone he met and though his life was abruptly cut short, at the young age of 27 he had already accomplished a lot and was one of the youngest qualified accountants of his generation. You will remain in our hearts and memory forever, sun re o aburo mi!

Acknowledgements

As I begin to reflect on the scale of this project. I am reminded of the collaborated effort of those who worked tirelessly behind the scenes to help me achieve my goal of writing this book a reality.

First I would like to thank my parents for the values they have instilled in me, their love and unwavering support over the years.

To my amazing children - Dami and Tumi, your love is my strength and your presence in my life makes the journey worthwhile, and inspires me to be the best role model that I can be.

To my editor and proof-reader - Haminder Sehmi, who was the first person to see my original manuscript, she devoted her spare time to the book and whilst she made her suggestions, she was still motivating and encouraging, which was quite useful for a newbie author like myself. Her input and attention to detail transformed my work into a great reference book for those that are looking for that extra boost to start and grow their own businesses.

I would like to thank Tinu Adeyemi, a colleague and friend, who has been a constant source of encouragement over the years and whenever we met her first words to me were usually "Mo, when are you going to write that book?"

To my good friend Segun Fajemisin, a renowned journalist, who supported and guided me through the complex process of getting this book published, his contributions and advice were invaluable.

I would like to thank my daughter Tumi and Karen West-Whylie for taking the time to do the final proofreading of the book and especially to Karen for her support.

To the participants who have attended my seminars, to my social media family and to all my clients - I have learned so much from you and acknowledge your participation in this work.

To all those who inspired me to follow my dreams by living theirs – Oprah Winfrey, Anthony Robbins, Robert Kiyosaki, Maya Angelou, Richard Branson and Les Brown.

A special thank you to Catherine Thomson, Mavis Amankwah, Ian Griffith, Dayo Olomu and Darren Rodwell for believing in me and giving me more opportunities to grow.

And finally thank you to the whole host of folk who have supported me on my journey, you all helped me to get my MOJO working, its impossible to thank everyone, but I am forever grateful to you - my friends, family and clients.

Foreword

When Mo Obadina approached me to write the forward of her book, I felt very honoured indeed as far as I am concerned, if anyone has earned the right to compose this book, it is surely her. This book emits a strong message to everyone and the message is clear. Get your business to the next level. I encourage you to read this book and I know you will not be able to put it down until you have reached the last word. It will indeed help your business stand out and succeed.

Cllr Sade Bright ~ Cabinet Member for Equalities & Cohesion, London Borough of Barking & Dagenham, (Author, Dream Big: Stretch Your Boundaries)

In this book, find out:
- Why and how to take action right now
- How to turn your idea into a business
- How to clarify your business vision and goals
- How to find customers and market your business
- How to make your business more profitable

Endorsements for Unleash your Business MOJO!

"The book is superb. Straight talking and straight to the point. Nothing complex about technology, social media or strategy, but some very simple home truths that are very difficult to argue against which is how a business should be built, using simple strategies. This book gave me a jolt as it reinforced my belief in entrepreneurship and taught me a few new things – in Social Media. This book is a must read for anyone in or thinking of starting a business."

Alfie Best ~ Chairman Wyldecrest Parks, The UK's number 1 Park Operator

---

"If you are looking for simple, yet powerful and productive facts on how to unleash your business mojo, then look no further. This is an ideal daily master class guide to that X-tra boost you have been looking for."

Anne Wafula Strike MBE ~
Teacher/Paralympian/Speaker/Author/International Disability Rights Advocate

---

"I am delighted to endorse "Unleash Your Business MOJO!" by Mo Obadina. Mo sets out the steps you need to take to set up your own business. Mo Obadina hasn't written a text book. Instead she takes us on her own journey and shares what worked and what didn't work. It will inspire those dreaming of running their own business but never finding the time to fulfill them."

Cllr. Darren Rodwell ~ *Leader of the Council, London Borough of Barking & Dagenham*

"On behalf of Barking Enterprise Centre I am delighted to support this book by Mo Obadina. All too often Business and Management books require a Masters' degree to understand the concepts, the reality is more people are looking to start their own business and a straight forward, no nonsense book filled with tested advice to start them on their journey can only enrich their opportunities. It's an easy to read business book packed with powerful tips."

Karen West-Whylie ~ *Chief Executive Officer, Barking Enterprise Centres*

"The book contains views on how to get started with one's ambition and making a success of business. A planned programme of how to go about such venture is very material and compulsory in order to be successful and get your business mojo working. Most businesses end up in the heart and head, since it is not stated in writing, and as such fails "ab initio." It is well known that there cannot be progress without vision and planning. This book helps you to achieve this by using a step by step strategy to ensure that your business has a better chance of success."

Chief Otunba Deru ~ President Institute of Chartered Accountants of Nigeria (2015/16)

"After reviewing the book **(Unleash Your Business MOJO!)** I believe that this book is an asset in itself for readers who want to be successful entrepreneurs. This book is a composition of steps taking you as a reader through different stages and preparations for the business i.e. from branding to marketing and keeping it consistent. It also has a pinch to it for all those who have always had a dream but were too afraid to pursue it, a motivational kick to make their dreams come true. I think this book is also helpful for business students to understand the basics of business from sixth form onwards as I believe it's the ideal age for ideas to blossom and Mo's book is ideal in terms of simplicity, vocabulary and structure.

Overall, an invaluable resource for new and existing entrepreneurs who want more exposure to chase up their dreams. I hope this book brings real life success stories for the

readers and serves as a light for those who would like to have a road map to their dream business. If you read this book and then take action, expect to see results!"
Barrister Gul Nawaz Khan ~ Director Addison and Khan Solicitors.

"One of the best things in life is to find the best ideal you need to progress in life. Mo has a unique talent that puts words of encouragement and ideas into people's minds. That is why this book is fantastic and has come at the right time, especially now that our diversities and cultures need to be connected for success into global markets as well as local markets."
Dr Alistair Soyode ~ Founder and Chair of Ben TV, Europe's First Ethnic-Oriented Television Channel

---

"At last, a book on the real truth about starting a profitable business sounds just up our street. In this book, Mo's quest would seem to prove that the system for building a profitable business model is not broken, however we need to use the tools recommended to self-correct, slowly evolve and step up. Truth of the matter is there are lots of voices around us, but you need to step away so you can hear your own voice again.

If you are seeking valuable tools in order to find your own voice again in today's pressured world of business, then this book is for you. Enjoy!"

Tinuola Adeyemi ~ Fellow Association of Chartered and Certified Accountants (FCCA)

"I have known Mo for a while now and she is honest, enthusiastic and passionate about her work as well as being professional, knowledgeable and insightful. All these qualities and more are felt when you read her book. Mo has gone from strength to strength over the years pushing herself and her self-belief that she will succeed and she has. There is no better person than Mo to have written this book, so if you are a new business or a business that has run out of ideas then this book will inspire and motivate you in your business."

Catherine Thomson ~ C&D Cleaning Services

"Mo's book is short, sharp, concise and captivates the essence of what modern business practices are about. Unleash Your Business MOJO is a must-read for entrepreneurs, would be business men and women and young people aspiring to become captains of industry in the future.

It offers the motivational and aspirational enthusiasm that provides people with that proverbial kick up the backside and introduces them to the possible challenges and sacrifices they will face in the drive to succeed. Furthermore, it lays emphasis on the need for perseverance, tenacity, staying power and belief if they want to reach the finish line.

As with any other trade or profession, learning the ropes can be challenging and beginners face an uphill task getting up the first few rungs of the ladder. This book offers them a beginner's introduction to the world of going it alone, acting as an all-in-one guide to business management, theory and strategy.

I for one enjoyed reading the book as it offers a roadmap to success and reading it could turn your life around. I recommend it."

Ayo Akinfe ~ Editor, Nigerian Watch.

CONTENTS

Your dream
It's never tool late to pursue your dream
The keys to a successful business
Is your passion burning?
Where to go for inspiration
Supersize your passion
The magic moment to start

Why you need a vision
Creating your business vision
Winning Companies with winning vision statements
Creating Your Business Vision

Introduction

Mo Obadina, the CEO of Mo's MOJO is an award winning business coach and chartered accountant. Mo's MOJO won an award at the Barking & Dagenham Chamber of Commerce Business Awards 2016. She is a Fellow of the Association of Certified Chartered Accountants (ACCA) and a member of the Institute of Chartered Accountants of Nigeria.

Having worked on several business programmes, where she analysed various businesses and their plans and supported well over 200 entrepreneurs. She was able to see that most plans were not written with a clear vision – indeed many of them were not even written by the business owner. Mo decided to bring her skills of business and accounting together to set up Mo's MOJO and also created the One Page Business Map - that shows all the key steps of running a successful business – Vision, Objectives and Marketing etc. on a single page.

"8 out of 10 entrepreneurs who start businesses fail within the first 18 months. A whopping 80% crash and burn due to poor planning."

"At Mo's MOJO our goal is always to exceed our clients' expectations. Mo's MOJO uses a number of tools including the hugely successful "One Page Business Map" to put the MOJO back into our clients businesses by helping them put their vision and strategies down on paper.

> *"Failing to plan is planning to fail."*
> *~ Benjamin Franklin[1]*

Mo has been on BEN TV and Colourful Radio as the resident business coach advising viewers on what it takes to be successful in business. She has also been featured in the press as a subject matter expert. She hosts a free monthly Women's Networking Meeting in her local area and is a popular keynote speaker. Mo has a strong presence on Facebook, LinkedIn and Twitter and her blog on www.mosmojo.com. features thought provoking posts on business development in a rapidly changing economic environment.

In her spare time Mo plays golf and enjoys roller-skating. She also contributes her time to local organisations and is the currently the Vice President of her local Women's Institute and a member of a few other local charities. She is currently working her way through her bucket list of 50 by 50 and invites you to join her on her adventures via social media.

---

[1]　*Benjamin Franklin, (O.S. 1705 – 1790) was one of the Founding Fathers of the United States. He was leading author, inventor and politician.*

Preface

I am so happy to be sharing my experiences and knowledge with you. I have wanted to write a book for as long as I can remember. It was always a childhood dream of mine. I was reading the Sunday newspapers and *Reader's Digest* by the time I was seven, but like many people something held me back from putting my thoughts on paper. I had that common feeling of doubt, "What will people say?" and all the other things we tell ourselves. So, I feel so blessed that you are now able to share this dream with me. And if there is anything that you have ever wanted to do and are still dreaming and worrying about, please don't tarry. Life is so short, and soon it will be time to say goodbye forever.

I'm glad that I decided to go ahead and write this book. And as you turn the pages, I hope I am able to awaken that MOJO within you that makes you want to pursue that dream of starting your business, growing your existing business, or even just sharing this with someone you know that is thinking of starting or growing their own business. It contains a step-by-step approach to what you need to start and grow your business, but you can dip in and out of the chapters, as you want.

When I started this business a few years ago I read a few books and went to seminars but still found it difficult, as people told you what to do but not what they did, that didn't work. In this book I try to talk about my mistakes as well as what I wish I'd known before I started my own business.

I have read well over 100 books, and I can tell you that most books leave a mark, no matter how small. I hope that this book leaves a big mark on your life and in your business.

Thanks for choosing to read this book and do keep me up to date with your business journey. I would also appreciate and value your constructive comments and honest feedback, so do email me at hello@unleashyourbusinessmojo.com or via social media.

For more resources please visit
www.unleashyourbusinessmojo.com

CHAPTER ONE

THE DREAM

"Concerning all acts of initiative (and
creation), there is one elementary truth, the
ignorance of which kills countless ideas and
splendid plans: that the
moment one definitely commits oneself,
then Providence moves too."
~ William Hutchinson Murray[2]

Your Dream

Most people who want to start a business have had
this burning desire to do so for as long as they can
remember. Did you have a childhood dream of
owning and running your own company? I know I certainly
did.

Growing up, my dad was the alpha and omega of the house:
everything started and stopped with him. If Dad didn't

---

[2]   *William Hutchison Murray (1913 – 1996) was a Scottish mountaineer and writer.*

rubber-stamp it, it wasn't happening. So it was a shock to me when, at 18, I went to do some work experience at my dad's workplace and realised that he had a manager, someone he had to report to. He was not the main guy! My reality changed that day and I told myself in that moment that I would never work for anyone else. When I became older, I wanted to be the boss.

I held on to that dream for many years, through lots of challenges and false starts, and finally I was able to do that just before I turned 40. Each time things get slow, as they do in business, and I feel like dusting off my CV to head off to the recruiters, I remind myself of that vision I had when I was 18.

So what did you dream of becoming when you were young?

> *"Life is either a daring adventure or nothing at all."* ~ Helen Keller[3]

It's never too late to pursue your dream

If you're like a lot of potential business owners and entrepreneurs, you are probably waiting for the right moment – but there isn't one! It could be that you're fed up of working for someone else, the children have left home and you have spare time on your hands, or your relationship has recently ended and you're looking for a boost to build up your self-

---

[3]　*Helen Adams Keller (1880 – 1968) was an American author, political activist, and lecturer.*

confidence and make money in the process – choose times like these to start – whatever it is, use it as an excuse to put your ideas and visions in to action.

There has never been a greater time to start a business. There are government loans available. If you're a woman there are many groups that support women to start a business and so there are a lot more women in business – which means that you have more role models, than say 10 years ago. It's so much easier than it used to be. There's free marketing via social media. This has made it possible for small businesses to go head-to-head with big businesses without having to have an unlimited advertising budget. All around us are inspiring women who have stepped out of their comfort zone to create great businesses to leave their mark on the world, and inspire people like us to stand up and be counted.

Did you know that a recession actually produces more millionaires than when the economy is vibrant?

If you are over 50 then you're in good company. There are quite a few well-known entrepreneurs who started their businesses well into their 50s. The founder of KFC started the company when he was 65. Ray Kroc bought and created the McDonald's franchise when he was 59. Arianna Huffington started *The Huffington Post* when she was 54! All over the world you will find evidence of late bloomers!

The biggest thing holding you back is not your age, but your mind-set. If you've already reached middle age and think you haven't achieved any entrepreneurial success, do not give up! It's easy to think that we don't feature on the map, when all we hear about are the Zuckerbergs who've achieved success while barely out of nappies. We're used to hearing that retiring is normal at around 65 years old, so we start mentally winding down in our 50s when, in fact, we should be starting to open ourselves up to new opportunities and growth, and possibly pursing those latent dreams we used to have and that still niggle at us.

Guess what? Today is the youngest you'll ever be!

> IDEAS: ideas are the starting point for any successful enterprise. But people have loads of them, and then just sit on them without doing anything.

"You don't have to be great to start, but you need to start to be great." ~ Zig Ziglar[4]

Is Your Passion Burning?

Passion: we hear this word bandied around a lot. There are books that talk about 'Passion to Profits' - in fact Amazon lists 412 publications under this genre. So if you can't beat 'em, you

---

[4]   *Hilary Hinton "Zig" Ziglar (1926 – 2012) was an American author, salesman, and motivational speaker.*

better join 'em! Turning passion into profits is the new buzz phrase, but let's look at the nitty gritty.

We all have passions, talents, skills, and some of them are unique to us alone. Believe me when I say that we are each blessed with the traits, backgrounds, parents and environments that make our talents and our take on the world unique to us. No one else has had the same experiences that you have had, so that makes you stand out. Now, it's about looking to find out what you have always held dear to you. Let me ask you these questions:

- Is there something you find yourself doing even when time is limited?
- Would you do it even if you weren't paid?
- If you had all the money in the world what would you be doing right now?
- When you look into the future, what have you promised yourself, that you would do when you retire? Maybe you promised yourself that you'd take some lessons in sewing, writing, or cooking, or even go back to school to study law.
- What's stopping you from doing it now?

Tomorrow you will be older, and so the years keep passing by - in a flash they're gone. Better to start now!

"We will either find a way or make one."
~ Hannibal [5]

---

[5] *Hannibal (247-183/181BC) Military Commander from Carthage.*

Is there something that's happened to you that always fires you up and makes you want to warn, educate, or inspire others about it? It could just be a parking ticket that you received. Yes, Bernie Segal was someone who got a parking ticket and went on to start a website, giving advice and support to other drivers who found themselves in similar situations. He has now written a book based on his knowledge of parking tickets. He monetized his website and developed a lucrative speaking career – all from getting a parking ticket! Isn't that a wonderful way to start a business? Moving from a place of pain to taking positive action.

Maybe you've been embroiled in a legal battle with a company, hospital or employer. You could use your experience to start educating others. It could even be a bad relationship. Rather than remember it and feel bad about it, get out and educate others. Help prevent them from making the same mistakes that you made. Turn it into a profit.

I once attended an event where the keynote speaker was a domestic violence trainer. She delivered training to the police, the Home Office and charitable organisations up and down the country on abuse within relationships. She had been in that kind of abusive relationship herself, but decided to use her experience as her career. She even went back to university to get the relevant qualifications to ensure she is seen as a leading authority in her field. This is great and it will endear her more to her listeners because she has personal experience of what she's talking about.

Is there something that you can do naturally, without giving much thought to it, something where your natural ability stands out because people always compliment you about it? For example, maybe you're good at connecting people, or the go-to expert for information about legal matters - you could write a 'how-to' manual about that. Maybe you have a unique talent in an unorthodox industry. Perhaps, a man who can do women's hair, or a woman who's good with cars. As I'm writing this, there's a woman on the radio talking about her blog - for Scotch egg recipes! How random is that? There's even a group called the Scotch Egg Appreciation Society - it has over 800 members. So come on, think about what you can create.

"The real magic of discovery lies not in seeking new landscapes but in having new eyes." ~ Marcel Provost[6]

Don't worry if you don't have enough knowledge in the area you're interested in. If you like to be supported by paper qualifications, you can do cheap courses online. There's Udemy or Lynda, you can get books on the subject area, or just do a lot of desk-based research. Google will reveal the answers you want if you interrogate it well.

---

[6] *Valentin Louis Georges Eugène Marcel Proust, (1871 – 1922) was a French novelist, critic, and essayist.*

The final test is - can you make money out of it? Before you answer that, picture this - 30 years ago if anyone had asked us whether we would pay for bottled water, there would have been a resounding NO. Who in their right mind would have bought water that you could get from the tap 30 years ago? That industry is now worth over $100 billion per year, and growing. So, can you make money from your passion? Test it out on the right people - You do need to be able to make some money from it, otherwise it's just an expensive hobby. So how do I get started?

The Key To A Successful Business

Well, starting is the key. Because if you don't start nothing happens. Some reasons why people don't start have been explored in other publications, but let's talk about the most common reasons here.

The number one reason is the fear of failure. This fear is unfounded, and although it can be real for those who experience it, it is packaged up as perfectionism, procrastination, fear of success, and all the common - 'Too old, too young, too beautiful' :) excuses we all have. You must feel the fear and do it anyway. What have you got to lose? Isn't it better to try and fail than not to try at all? How would you feel in 20 years' time if you had had the chance to start a business, but you chose to ignore it because you were scared? Imagine sitting in your rocking chair and being asked by your grandchild or younger self for advice on whether to start a business or follow a dream. What would you tell them? So, why don't you take that advice yourself? (Assuming you told them to go ahead. If not, well, I would love to know what you did tell them!)

A second reason might be lack of money or funds. But is this really a reason not to start? The world is littered with people who started their businesses with nothing at all, only an idea and a commitment to make it happen. Humble beginnings and a poor background are actually great motivators for success. Take the CEO of WhatsApp, Jan Koum. He's a perfect example of this, he moved to California with his mother and spent his teenage years in social housing. He is now a billionaire having sold WhatsApp to Facebook. So are the Starbucks' founder and chairman, Howard Schultz, who grew up in a housing estate for the poor, and Oprah who was born into a poor family in Mississippi. Check out this article – you'll find some gems there: Successful people who failed.[7]

Where to go for inspiration

The top three industries predicted to produce the next wave of millionaires and billionaires are: agriculture and food, training and development, and health and beauty (a famous US family monopolise this!). And think of all the business ideas centred around these industries that include: communications, leadership, motivation, marketing, social

---

[7] *http://www.huffingtonpost.com/2015/01/16/19-successful-people-who-failed_n_6438868.html - Retrieved 14th July 2016*

media management, boutique travel, analysis of information, data security, supplies etc. You can start a business or write a book on any of these areas too.

Yes, this information might be all over Google, but if you have ever tried to write an article about a subject, have you noticed how long it takes to do the research? People have scarce resources, and time is one of them, so they will be willing to pay to get all that information in one place - either on a website or in a book. I buy books, not because I can't use Google for the information that I want, but sometimes I haven't got the time. I gain more from books, I can bookmark them and can also go back and get more information from that book. How many web pages have you bookmarked or 'evernoted' for later, but never remembered to go back to? This is why a book is better.

Remember, you are not aiming to create a business for everyone but just a group of people. This is sometimes called a 'niche[8]', although it's a hard thing for start-ups to grasp. I do understand this because I was once in that position myself. You can feel like you're leaving money on the table if you don't cater for everyone that stops by your office asking for a solution to their problem. But let's face it, you can't meet everyone's needs: your funds are limited, and even if you could

---

[8]　*Concentrating all marketing efforts on a small but specific and well defined segment of the population. Niches do not 'exist' but are 'created' by identifying needs, wants, and requirements of a particular market segment – www.businessdictionary.com (July 2016)*
Read more: http://www.businessdictionary.com/definition/niche-marketing.html#ixzz4FWlbkRa2

afford to advertise, you still need the resources to meet all those people's needs. If you're just starting out, it's helpful if you identify an area and stick with it.

"The biggest single barrier to the development of an effective strategy is the belief that a company has to appeal to the entire market." ~ Al Ries[9]

Resources: Examples of 100 business ideas on my website: www.unleashyourbusinessmojo.com

Supersize your Passion

Now that you have decided on your passion, it's time to craft it and make it valuable to your new and potential customers. If it's a profession that requires you to stand up and speak, like being a trainer or facilitator, then you may have to do more work, depending on your level of experience. We are all able to speak in front of our friends with great ease. We can all stand up and we can all speak. However, when it comes to doing both at once, we become tongue-tied. Research proves over and over again that being buried alive is considered a better option by some of us than having to stand up and speak - how interesting!

---

[8]   *Al Ries (Born: November 14, 1926, US) is a marketing professional and author.*

We have all listened to great speakers, good speakers, and those who appear disorganised. What you must do now is to start looking at how others in your industry package and deliver their speeches, and try to see how you can polish your own good skills. You will have to invest time in putting all your knowledge together, but please do not spend too much time on this. Read a few books on the subject area, attend seminars on those topics, and don't worry about it being perfect right now. It will evolve anyway, and your customers will give you the feedback you need to develop your material further.

The Magic Moment to Start?

As I've mentioned before do not wait for the right time. The only way to get better at business is to be in business. You still need to do some research, though. There will be other experts out there that are doing similar things to what you do - check them out, and look at how they deliver their knowledge, look at their sales funnel i.e. how they promote, attract and sell to their audiences. Having the knowledge is one thing, being able to promote it is another. As you create your services or products, remember that you are trying to solve a problem: you are creating a solution to your audience's problems or challenges.

You can look at other systems, but make sure that you develop your own solution framework, giving it your own brand and acronym. We have examples:

- The Abraham Maslow Hierarchy of Needs
- 7 Habits of Highly Effective People
- The 4 P's

Make sure you create a model, strategy or process that is unique to your business. It's your unique selling point, and it is imperative to success. My business exploded when I used that, and the One Page Business Map that I created is what my 90-minute seminars are based on. It's a model that works for me. Your strategy or framework is what everything you do will be based on - training programmes and seminars, your advice, even writing a book. And systems are easy to replicate and teach, so you can create it once and leverage it forever. Think about 'Rich Dad Poor Dad', a book that has spurned a multimillion-dollar empire. So has Steve Covey, of the 7 Habits fame.

CHAPTER TWO

THE VISION

Having a vision is a joy. In fact, the greatest gift to mankind is not the gift of sight, but the gift of vision. So let's start with the end in mind. Where exactly do you see yourself in three years' time? Take a good look around and you will see that the ability to look is common: we can all do it. However, the ability to see is rare - and the tiny number of true leaders and visionaries around us confirms this.

Your Vision

Before we go any further, let's think for a minute about this thing called vision. What is it? According to the Oxford Dictionary, it is *"the ability to think about or plan the future with imagination or wisdom."*

Being a visionary means that you have to imagine the future, sometimes without any reference points. Think of the Wright brothers, those who built the Great Pyramids of Egypt, the computer hardware and software inventors, even what you're sitting on now (if you are!) was once someone's vision - they all had to take a leap of faith and work hard, not only to make their visions understood but to bring them to reality. And we're now lucky enough to benefit from their vision, consistent action and unwavering commitment.

Why do you need a Vision?

It is very important to have a vision because it is at the heart of our lives and everything we do. It's like a roadmap to our life. Setting off on a journey, you wouldn't dream of getting into your car without a map or an idea of your final destination, so why do so many of us continue to live our lives without a clear vision?

A life without a vision is a poor one, and a person who has a vision but cannot pursue it is a frustrated person. A vision gives us a reason to live, and if we have no vision there really is no great future to look towards. We are all unique and endowed with different talents and dreams - we owe it to ourselves and others to pursue them.

"Our deepest fear is not that we are inadequate. Our deepest fear is that we are powerful beyond measure. It is our light, not our darkness that most frightens us. We ask ourselves, who am I to be brilliant, gorgeous, talented, fabulous? Actually, who are you not to be? You are a child of God." ~ Marianne Williamson[10]

---

[10] *Marianne Deborah Williamson (born Jul. 1952) is an American spiritual teacher, author and lecturer.*

Winning Companies with winning vision statements:
Let's look at some companies that have had tremendous
success by having a great vision:

Walt Disney
Vision: To make people happy

Nike
To crush Adidas

Stanford University
To be the Harvard of the West

Wal-Mart Inc.
To generate $125 billion revenue by 2000 (actual revenue:
$200 billion)

In the next section, let's begin...

Creating Your Business Vision
*"The things you do for yourself are gone
when you are gone, but the things you do
for others remain as your legacy."*
~ Kalu Ndukwe Kalu[11]

Now it's time to breathe life into your own business vision.
This exercise will take just 10 minutes. So grab a pen and a
sheet of paper, and find a quiet place to sit.

---

[11]   *Kalu N. Kalu (born Sept. 1954) is associate professor of political science at Auburn
University at Montgomery.*

Doing this exercise will help you to see the vision for your business that is already within you. Imagine that there are no barriers - money, age, location, health, and fear of success or failure – there's nothing to stop you.

Just write - or draw, paint, make a collage - whatever you feel comfortable with. Just make sure you get your vision down on paper.

Imagine that you're 90 years old and you decided to throw a party to mark this great milestone. You're surrounded by your loved ones and business associates, now I want you to picture the life you live and the business that you've created - You're happy, healthy, and proud that your business has been very successful. (Tip: imagine that you - or your business - have won awards, been featured on the Forbes rich list, in national and international press and been invited to share your wisdom etc.) A reporter from a national paper comes up to you during the party to interview you about your life and asks you following questions, how would you respond?

1. What goals have you been able to fulfil due to the success of your business? (i.e. financial, personal development, business, relationship, fitness and spiritual goals)
2. What difference has your business made to your customers/clients and the community?
3. What legacy would you or your business like to leave? (How would you like to be remembered?)

Try and write about your business in the present tense - as if it has already happened. And remember, you are 90 years old now!

There are some examples online at
www.unleashyourbusinessmojo.com

How was that? I hope you did the exercise. If you didn't, do go back and do it now because we're going to start taking action towards...

CHAPTER THREE

THE ROADMAP
TO SUCCESS

"Though no one can go back and make a brand-new start, anyone can start from now and make a brand-new ending."
~ Unknown[12]

Well, now that you've crafted your own vision, let's start looking at the steps you will need to take to achieve it.

Setting Goals

Goals are like a roadmap to achieving your vision. They help by breaking it down into baby steps: things you can do one at a time, with each one moving you closer to your vision.

Here's another tip: research has shown that people who write their goals down have a greater chance of achieving them.

---

[12] *First mentioned in the 1982 book – Rejection by James R. Sherman, Chapter: How to Survive Rejection, Quote Page 45, Published by Pathway Books, Minnesota.*

With my clients, I like to start working backwards, using *year three* goals as a starting point. The reason why we go for the longer-term goals first is that we often underestimate what we can achieve in the longer term, while we overestimate what we can accomplish in the short term. We do that all the time. Just take a look at your to-do list - if you have one. It's probably populated with things that have been on it for a while, and I bet at the time you wrote it you thought you'd accomplish them all on *that* day.

> **"Record the vision
> And inscribe it on tablets,
> That the one who reads it may run."
> Habakkuk 2:2**[13]

Medium-Term Goals

Let's take a look at the numbers. How much will the business be making in three years' time? How many staff will you have? How many product lines or ranges will you have? How many shops will stock your products? Which part of the country will you be located in? What will your profit margin be? How will you grow the business - organically, through takeovers, or by external investment?

---

[13]   *New American Standard Bible Copyright ©1960, by The Lockman Foundation, La Habra, Calif.*

Here are a couple of examples to show you what I mean.

A year in Focus

Your medium term goal could be: by the end of December 2017, I will have started my business as a shoe retailer.

You could break that down into smaller goals. For example, by January 2017 I will have completed my One Page Business Map. By March 2017, I will have done all the surveys and research into the product lines and designs I will offer. By June 2017, I will start sourcing manufacturers and place my orders; I will also start building the business website and start working on my marketing. Your launch date could then be in December 2017.

Drilling down

A three-year goal broken down first into a 12-month goal and then a three-month goal is a good place to start from. For instance, say you want to achieve sales of £50k by year three. This means that in year one you will probably aim for £12k, which easily breaks down into £1k a month and £250 a week. This is easier to grapple with than saying you want to make £50k in three years all in one go.

It's the same if you want 100 clients at the end of a 12-month period. You will need to break that down to say eight a month, which becomes two a week. These bite-sized goals are easier for you to achieve.

Short-Term Goals

Now that we've worked out our three-year goals, we can move on to the goals we want to achieve in the short term. What do you want your company to have achieved in 12 months' time? Take a closer look at the numbers above and break them down further.

So if you want to achieve £75k at the end of year three then perhaps you can aim for £30k at the end of year one. Remember that numbers don't necessarily triple over three years, although there can be a cumulative effect, for example starting with £10k p.a. and then reaching £60k by year three. Just look at all the goals you have for 3 years' time and divide them into smaller goals over the three-year period.

Finally, now look at your three-month goals. This will depend very much on how much work you have done and what stage you are at with your business. If you are brand spanking new some of your goals will be practical, like getting in place a website, promotional material, product pricing, packaging, an office address, and clients; doing market research for clients and suppliers; and working out how and where to sell – in other words, a marketing strategy to make sure that the money does actually come in.

"It's estimated that only 3-4% of the population have written goals and its interesting that by retirement only 4% of us have acquired enough wealth to maintain our income levels and quality of life" and according to a study done by Gail Matthews at Dominican University, those who wrote down their goals accomplished significantly more than those who did not write down their goals.

Once you have sorted out the goals, you may want to look at your mission. Whilst your vision is in the future, your mission is what keeps you doing what you do every single day. Don't worry if you don't have a mission: some of the biggest companies in the world struggle with this one and normally amalgamate the vision and mission together. Just do what works for you, and make sure it keeps you on track to realise your vision.

Get a FREE copy of my goal-setting template at www.unleashyourbusinessmojo.com.

If you don't have time to write your goals down, where will you find the time to accomplish them?

Don't be a Lone Ranger - Get Support

A crucial part of setting and achieving goals is sharing them with others. If you are brave enough, you can put them online and hold yourself accountable to others that way. After years of struggling and failing to write this book I decided to take drastic action. In September 2015, I sent out a veiled goal to my mailing list promising to finish my book by December

2015. Subsequently, I entered the NaNoWriMo competition, which is a global race among authors to complete 50,000 words during the month of November. I used this to propel myself towards my goal of getting my book written and published. And voila! You are now reading it. To make my goal even more achievable, I set up a group of like-minded authors to ensure that we supported each other to hit the target.

Getting a coach or mentor to support you is also a great way to ensure that you achieve your goals. Weight Watchers use this to a great advantage, getting people to come together and set weight loss goals. So do sports coaches, who help athletes like Usain Bolt to achieve greater levels of fitness so that they can continually exceed their targets. I also have a coach who ensures that I walk my talk and deliver greater results than if I just did it all by myself. I can hold you accountable to your goals, if you want me to.

Another vital ingredient is...

Your Mind-set: Self-Belief and Confidence

To really have a vision and pursue it we must have a strong belief in ourselves. You must believe that you are a rare gem and that there has never been nor ever will be anyone like you. Your DNA is unique, your fingerprints are unique, and so are you. This is true!

I understand that having a strong belief in yourself is not as easy as it sounds, especially at the start of a new business or when undertaking unfamiliar tasks. Just remember that it's normal, and you must just feel the fear and do it anyway.

There are loads of reasons or excuses for having self-doubt - we are taught not to fail, so we fear failure. We are surrounded by people who are scared to try, and it rubs off on us. Which four people (bar family members) do you commonly spend your quality time with? If they're not where you want to be, they could be holding you back. We feel comfortable among people who are like us and we don't like challenging the status quo – this means that *your* friends may not always encourage you into self-employment. When I wanted to start out alone, I had friends tell me that I was better off in a secure job, but I did eventually break away from the norm - and you can too. Sometimes though, we need a degree of doubt, because beginning a new venture with a hundred per cent belief in success may not give us enough motivation to start moving. For some of us there will need to be a degree of doubt to challenge and propel us forward. Perhaps you could cast your mind back to a person who told you that you couldn't do something - and then try and prove them wrong! I once heard someone say, "Don't envy, be envied." It might sound odd, but remember Nike's vision? They used it to get to where they are now, so it works!

Success leaves Clues

You have to remember that everyone has doubts about themselves, even the most successful people. Mariah Carey, the multi award-winning singer worth millions, was once heard saying, "I've always had really low self-esteem, and I still do."

The late award-winning author Maya Angelou said, "I have written eleven books, but each time I think, Uh oh, they're going to find out now. I've run a game on everybody, and they're going to find me out."

And here's Mike Myers: "At any time I still expect that the no-talent police will come and arrest me."

So there you go. You can see that self-doubt is universal; so don't let it stop you from achieving your dreams.

One thing that helps to reinforce my self-belief is to write down my strengths and achievements and keep the list to hand. When I feel down, I read through it, and it makes me feel inspired and ready to face the day. I also use music, and two of my favourite get-up-and-go songs are "Something Inside So Strong" by Labi Siffre and "Ain't No Stoppin' Us Now" by McFadden & Whitehead. Which songs make your heart sing and inspire you? Put them on your playlist now, and begin to build your confidence and self-belief.

*"I am the greatest. I said that even before
I knew I was. I figured that if I said it
enough, I would convince the world that I
really was the greatest."*
~ Mohammed Ali[14]

MOJO Hacks:

- Your vision can be as dramatic as you want it to be. Just remember that it has to inspire your stakeholders - customers, staff and investors - to believe in it. Everything you do as a business should tie into your vision
- Make yourself accountable to friends, a master group, or a coach
- Write down your goals as though you are on a fun and exciting journey, like being part of your bucket list, such as, '30 goals to achieve before I'm 30' or '50 by 50' or 'my 12 goals this year' Anything that adds juice and can propel you towards your vision is good. I have my '50 before 50' bucket list, which I talk about on my blog
- Make sure your goals are SMART. Every goal must be specific, measurable, achievable, realistic, and have a time frame
- Be focused. Make sure you keep your goals where you can see them, and adapt them where necessary
- If you're a visual person, like me, then translate your goals into pictures using a vision board. (Read more about a Vision board at www.unleashyourbusinessmojo.com)

Now its time to look at why any sane person would choose self-employment...

---

[14] *Muhammad Ali (born Cassius Marcellus Clay, Jr., January 17, 1942 – June 3, 2016) was an American Olympic and professional boxer and activist.*

CHAPTER FOUR

ROUTES TO SELF-EMPLOYMENT

"Don't be afraid to give up the good to go for the great." ~ John D. Rockefeller[15]

What you need to know about Self Employment

Self-employment could be a step towards becoming an entrepreneur and building a business that works for you. It can create jobs for others and allow you to do what you want, when you want, with a cushy pension to fall back on. Hopefully!

A lot of people who choose to go self-employed do so because of the perceived lifestyle, the freedom, and possibly the desire to become obscenely wealthy.

---

[15] *John Davison Rockefeller Sr. (1839 – 1937) was an American industrialist and philanthropist.*

In the UK there are more people in self-employment now, than at any point over the past 40 years. Though the reality is that they work longer hours and earn 40% less than their employed counterparts. There are over 4.5 million of us in self-employment in the UK - and together we make up nearly 15% of the total number of people in employment. Nearly half of all businesses close within their first three years of operation. Despite these startling statistics, many of us want to be our own boss. There are many ways into self-employment which I will cover under three broad headings.

Assisted self-employment

This is a soft landing into going it alone. The most common type is a franchise, where you get all the initial business support you need and a system to follow, which is fool proof. If you can read and are coachable then you will succeed, and the figures support this. Franchises have a 90% success rate compared to all other businesses. However, the entry costs are high, with the more established ones demanding up to £200,000 for set-up costs plus additional monthly fees. Smaller franchises are available for less than £10,000, so do shop around and make sure you get testimonials from existing franchisees - visit them and ask questions.

Visit https://www.thebfa.org/ https://www.franchiseinfo.co.uk/ http://www.franchisedirect.co.uk/ for information and guidance.

The other main type of assisted self-employment is network marketing - also known as multi-level marketing (MLM). This is a big arena for people who are going it alone; however statistics show that it has the highest failure rate, with over

90% of members making less than £3,500 a year (Source: *Business Students Focus on Ethics US*).

MLM spans many industries from beauty to health & fitness to groceries and coin collecting. You make money by selling the products/services and recruiting new members. If this is the route that you decide to take, you need to be self-motivated and organised to do this. Make sure that they have a great system of support in place which will depend on which team you join, so choose your team wisely. It could mean the difference between success or failure.

Virtual Entrepreneurs

These are the new breed of entrepreneurs. They're generally consultants or retailers that have used the Internet and technology to leverage their businesses to reach and service markets in virtually every part of the world. They include coaches, writers/bloggers, accountants, YouTubers/vloggers, SEO/web designers, EBay/Amazon sellers and marketing affiliates. With just a smart phone and a website you could be in business too! Social media, together with a good marketing strategy, can be a powerful tool to build an online business.

Scalable Businesses (Start Ups)

These have the potential to become big - really BIG: the future Facebook, Amazon, Virgin or Google. They all started very small, with little funding but a lot of hard work and tons of vision.

With this type of business, you start small and work through trial and error to create a proven product with a proven business model. You then get investors to provide the finance for the resources you need to take your products and services into new markets and geographical areas.

These entrepreneurs take big risks because the success rate is quite low - Remember the dot.com bubble? When they make it, everyone wishes they were in it from the get-go. Silicon Valley - the Las Vegas of the technology world - still has a failure rate of 90%! However, when you win, its payday! Remember, it isn't just about having a good idea or a product; it's how you market it. What's your USP? (unique selling point). Cue my One Page Business Map...which helps you identify the key stages required when starting a new business or project.

In the midst of all this remember to do your...

Research: How and Where to Do It

If you can't afford to pay people like me to help you, don't worry; there are a few places you can go to get specialist advice. Going online is probably the first choice for many, but there is a little place in the heart of London, which has a vast amount of resources that you simply cannot find online. The good news is that you can access some of these resources for free. The City Business Library has reports, information on trends and profiles for virtually any industry, with the contact details of nearly 100 million companies worldwide, 3 million of which are UK based. It holds information on the right marketing and promotional tools to reach your target audience. It also holds financial information that will be crucial to your new business. So if you live near London, let that be one of your main pit stops.

If you want to sell a physical product, then you will have to decide on a few more things:

- What is your great product idea?
- Are you clear about the branding, look and feel of the product?
- Are there similar ones on the market?
- Do you want to produce or manufacture the product yourself?
- Or will you just buy it and sell it on under your own brand (white label)?
- Will you sell your product from a physical location? Online? Or both? And if you're going to sell it online what sales routes will you use? Via your own website or other portals like EBay, Amazon or Etsy?

You will need to think about the appearance of the product, the packaging, production costs, selling price, availability, marketing, and the target market the product is aimed at. This involves some research, and you will also have to look at the wider market in terms of trends, demands and market size, as well as what stage of the life cycle your product is at. You can use something called the Ansoff Matrix to do this. This highlights the different stages that a product occupies during its life cycle.

The temptation to give up to soon

When should you give up?

One client was so frustrated one day that she called me up lamenting about how she was fed up with her business and was going to throw in the towel. My immediate response was, "I didn't know you had a towel to throw in." Of course that interrupted her thought pattern, and we were able to identify the bottlenecks in her business and get her moving forward again. It's always too early to stop, and fear is no excuse not to go on. Yes, you need to 'Feel the fear and do it anyway' Stop living in your comfort zone; magic doesn't happen there, it only happens outside of it ... stretch yourself.

Don't give up too soon. We all know that phrase: "Quitters never win and winners never quit." It really is just like that. If you have a vision you owe it to yourself to press ahead with it. No one else can deliver your dream and vision like you can, and no one wants it more than you do. So forge ahead, and remember the reason why you want it each time the road gets tough, you feel alone, or you get a 'no' when you were so sure of a 'yes'. Keep going and remind yourself that had Edison stopped after 9,000 attempts would we have light? Had Colonel KFC stopped after 1000 rejections nor would we have KFC? So let's get creative and think of...

Some Business Ideas

There are so many different ideas to choose from - your own or you could borrow someone else's idea and just improve or repackage it. Getting your idea to work will depend on your passion, skills, vision, the amount of money you have at your disposal, and how much money you want to make.

Is it a passion or something that you've always wanted to do? Perhaps you want to create a new product or service. What does it look like?

You might want to offer a subscription to an online portal or magazine like LinkedIn, Netflix and Audible. Or you could start a group on Facebook and find ways to monetise it.

It could be a new twist to an existing product or service – like Apple (MP3 players), Starbucks (Gourmet Coffee) or Ciroc (Vodka with new packaging) - all of which are old products repackaged.

You could buy into someone else's model, for example franchising or network marketing, food outlets, cleaning companies, recruitment agencies or health and beauty products.

Or you could create a portal/place/network where people can buy and sell – think of Amazon, Etsy, or eBay.

You can provide products or services that can be rented, leased or licensed – your expertise, cars, cameras, consultancy and training packages.

Start Small But Think BIG

Have great ideas, but spend wisely at the start-up stage.

Often, you're much better off looking for a business concept that is already doing well. Then take that idea, but do something different and better with it. Many great businesses are not peddling fresh ideas, just re-branding what is already out there and adding a new angle - MP3s then iPods, bottled water then Perrier, and permanent markers then Sharpies. Get the picture? Add a USP to it. Make it stand out. It could be just the branding, customer service, or even the pricing - Apple did this successfully!

Starting a new concept can be costly because you have to create an awareness of it, as well market and sell it.

Don't be afraid to stand on the shoulders of giants. Websites like Amazon, Alibaba, AliExpress, Etsy and eBay have done the hard work for you by building an audience for you to sell to - all around the globe! No expensive shop premises or legal agreements to worry about. Even YouTube lets you have your very own TV channel.

There are people on YouTube turning over thousands of pounds every year just from adverts placed on their videos that is based on the number of views that they have as well as the number of subscribers to their channels. And all most of them are doing is talking about their lives and their passions – make up, comedy sketches, making clothes, motivational topics, fishing, farming and the list goes on.

Of course, dream big: have bodacious visions of where you want your business to be in one, two, or three years' time. Dream big, but be prudent with your costs – both overheads and operating costs - until you can afford not to be. Do not let the lack of finances stop you from pursuing your dream. It is often said that the 'why' you are doing it is more important than the 'how' to do it. We have all read about businesses that started up with practically nothing - Amazon started from a garage, Facebook from a college dormitory. Don't buy it if you can rent it, and if you can borrow it why rent it?

Larry Ellison, one of the wealthiest people in the world, with a fortune worth $48 billion, co-founded Oracle with two partners and a total investment of $2,000; $1,200 was out of his own pocket.

It's much easier to choose a familiar product and add a twist to it, than trying to introduce a radically new product or service. The former requires fewer steps, less hard work, and far less outlay in marketing. Introducing a new product requires you to educate the customer, and to introduce a need that they haven't thought of yet. Both of these things require a lot of marketing and advertising, which costs money - and if you're reading this book it's probably something you haven't got lots of! Here are some ideas.

MOJO Hacks:

- If your business name stands out, it's memorable, and people will never forget you or your product/ service
- Sponsor or get your name on a big local event. Donate your product to raffles at such events too
- Team up with others. There's an African saying: 'If you want to go fast go alone, but if you want to go far go with others.' Don't be a lone ranger
- Give samples and information to people when you go to big events
- Aim to look for groups of people to promote to. Remember the lone ranger analogy? Find a herd that's your target audience, and try and sell to them. I prefer to hold short seminars introducing my One Page Business Map, rather than trying to talk to people one-on-one. It's a better use of my time

When you decide to go into business you must be willing to make this happen, and that takes a different skill set to being an employee. The buck really starts and stops with you.

CHAPTER FIVE

WHAT IT TAKES?

"Twenty years from now you will be more disappointed by the things that you didn't do than by the ones you did do. So throw off the bowlines. Sail away from the safe harbour. Catch the trade winds in your sails. Explore. Dream. Discover."
~ Mark Twain[16]

Are you a Risk Taker?

You must show initiative and be able to spot new opportunities in the market. You must also be a risk taker and have the ability to take rejection - not all your business moves will get positive results. Small businesses are plentiful in the UK. Over 96% of UK businesses are micro, i.e. they have fewer than nine employees, and over 500,000 of these were registered in 2014. The bad news is that over 250,000 close down every year.

---

[16] *Samuel Langhorne Clemens (1835 – 1910), better known by his pen name Mark Twain, was an American author and humourist.*

Consider the reasons why you want to set up your own business. People who do take that stance and go it alone mostly succeed because they believe in themselves, do a lot of research and planning, and are consistent and determined. Have you got what it takes to be like that? Do you see the glass as half full or half empty? What do you think are the pros and cons of self-employment?

What effect will starting your business have on your personal life and your family? How will it help you to achieve your vision or long-term goals?

You have to keep learning when you're in business. You have to have a strong belief in yourself and always showing up when no one else does. Remember Dyson had over 5,000 prototypes before he came up with the bagless vacuum cleaner. No, you're not creating a masterpiece for the world, but it is your masterpiece nonetheless. So be and do your best. So now let's …

SWOT Your Strengths

Well now that you've decided that you want to start a business, you may want to take an inventory of your skills. Let's look at the qualities you need to start a business, because it does take a certain type of person with a certain set of skills to start and stay in business. It's a tough road, and it's not always a straight one; there will be U-turns, cross roads and one-way streets, and times when it will seem like there's no way out. But the mind-set you adopt along this journey will ensure that you get to your destination. There will be trials, but as long as you are committed, have a plan and anticipate some of the challenges, you can make it happen.

The one thing you must have is focus, and the one way to achieve this is to have a plan - a plan of action that will include what you intend to achieve in the long term - your vision - and a road map of how to get there. I advise that once you've created your vision you set some goals for how you want to go about achieving that vision.

Do you have what it takes?

The skills it takes to run a business must be part of your strengths. At the end of this chapter there's a SWOT tool that you can use to identify what you are good at - SWOT is an acronym for Strengths, Weaknesses, Opportunities and Threats. In the beginning there may be tasks that you don't like doing but which you may have to do until you can afford someone who can do them for you, or have more clarity about what your business needs to do to succeed.

One of your strengths might be selling, whilst a weakness might be admin, but in the beginning you will have to do the admin yourself. Doing the admin is not a bad thing because you become more aware of what tasks need to be done. It might be worthwhile making an organisational chart with roles and duties. It doesn't matter whether all the roles are filled at this point because remember this is about your vision, and you can fill those roles as you go along. Be thorough with this exercise and be sure to list <u>all</u> your strengths and weaknesses. You might want to ask someone to do it with you because you may not be fully aware of your strengths.

Your weaknesses are probably things that you already know, but remember you can always turn these into strengths by reading up on them or taking a course. There are places like Udemy that run practically any course you can think of on the skills needed for business. Lynda and YouTube are the same. Virtually anything can be learned. Don't get carried away though; you only need to learn enough to start your business.

> *"...But the will must be stronger than the skill." Muhammad Ali*

What are your key:

Strengths?

These are characteristics that give your business an advantage over others.

- What are you offering and how does it differentiate you from your competitors?
- What do others perceive as your strengths?

Weaknesses?

These are characteristics that place the business at a disadvantage relative to others.

- What do your competitors do better than you?
- What do others perceive as your weaknesses?

Opportunities?

- What elements of your business could you exploit to its advantage?
- What are the trends or conditions that might positively impact you?

Threats?

- Are there elements in the environment that could cause trouble for your business? What are they?
- What trends or conditions might negatively impact you?

Resources: go to www.unleashyourbusinessmojo.com for a free copy of the SWOT form.

Mojo Task: Fill it in and send it to hello@unleashyourbusiness.com for a review and a free 15-minute consultation.

So now that you've filled in your SWOT analysis, it's time to...

Choose Your Target Audience

The people or organisations you want to sell your service or product to are very important - they are your target audience. Being able to identify a target audience to sell your product or service to makes it easier for you to market to them.

Once you've decided on your target audience, you will need to research this group in great detail in terms of what they do, where they live, where they go on holiday, the books or publications they read, their interests etc. The more you know about them, the easier it will become to market to them using language they understand and using the channels that they're more likely to use.

In choosing an audience, think of the people and the business that you have the most affinity with, the ones who possibly already know you, thus making it easier for you to sell to them. Starting a business is a tough journey. Make that journey easier by bringing along familiar faces as customers. Choose your audience, and then study their pains: what keeps them up at night? What results do they want? Or what does success look like to them? Then see how you can offer them solutions with your knowledge. Timing, and how you deliver and package your products, will be the keys to your success.

For example, if you are a caterer specialising in wedding cakes, we can assume the following about your target audience: the brides are on average 25-35 years old; they like bars and good restaurants; they travel; they're on social media, especially

YouTube, Facebook and Instagram; they probably read the Metro and bridal magazines; and they will attend bridal shows. So you can interact with them via these channels. This is how you go about identifying and targeting a particular group or audience. It's simple, but it's not easy because many find it difficult to sell to just one group. And just because you sell to one target market doesn't mean you can't sell to others - just make sure that you target that "ideal client" and that you appeal to others too. For example, Apple's marketing is targeted towards young people, but there are many people outside of this target market who use Apple products. They're aspirational products. It's the same with perfumes.

Resources: go to www.unleashyourbusinessmojo.com for a free copy of the Ideal Client Profile.

Mojo Task: Fill it in and send it to hello@unleashyourbusiness.com for a review and a free 15-minute consultation.

CHAPTER SIX

GETTING STARTED

What would you attempt to do if you knew you would not fail?" ~ Robert Schuller

If you're going through this book chronologically, you should have achieved the following by now:

- Created your compelling vision
- Written down your goals
- Done a SWOT analysis
- Filled out the Ideal Client Form

Great - well done for completing all the tasks! Now you're about to start taking real action.

Tips for Choosing a Business Name either Online or Offline

What's in a name? A lot! The domain name www.insurance.com sold for $35.6 million in 2010, and Apple apparently bought www.icloud.com for over $4 million in 2011.

Coca Cola, McDonald's, MTV, Google, Microsoft, MGM, Mercedes and Nike are some of the most recognised brands (and logos) in the world.

The name you choose for your business must be memorable and easy to pronounce. Come up with some names with friends and family, even your potential customers. Think of the words that describe your product and service, and use a thesaurus to get creative. Do not rush this step, because it could make or break your business, but do give yourself a deadline so that you don't spend too long on it. Look around online. The fewer syllables there are, the easier it will be to pronounce and find using the Internet search engines. Remember that, in this era, any name you choose will require a website, so make sure that it's clear too - avoid numerical substitutions if you can, don't use 4 instead of four, and try to keep it hyphen and dash free!

If you can, let your name say something about what you sell as well, although this may make it too wordy. But remember, your products can be named differently, so don't get too hung up on the business name.

Do buy your own domain name where you can. Don't piggyback on a host's website, such as Vistaprint, Moonfruit or Blogger, because this will make it difficult for you to have control over the optimisation of the website and to ensure there's flexibility in its appearance. Nowadays, every business is online, so there's a plethora of websites out there - both the obscure and the very well known - so try and distinguish your website by the domain name as well as the address. The first-level websites are the ones ending in .com, .gov, .net and .org. If you want to be internationally known, then .com is the way to go. But if you are a local brand with most of your customers being local then you can keep the domain local too, i.e.. co.uk. Check out places like www.domainsuperstar.com to find previously registered but now available websites.

MOJO Hacks:

- Come up with a name or ask others. You can set up a WhatsApp group and do it that way, or go online using Facebook
- Which logos do you like? Look online for inspiration
- You can get a new logo done or refresh your current logo on sites like PeoplePerHour or Fiverr if you're on a budget. Be sure to try more than one person so you get a choice

Your Checklist: To get moving...

Put together a list of what you need to get off the ground. The basic items, which I assume you have, are a laptop and Internet connection. Having a network of people to support you is of course a bonus (but, don't worry, you can even create that!) In fact, a lot of people have created a business purely by working online. The suitcase entrepreneur, the laptop entrepreneur, and a whole host of other online marketers have created great wealth by working almost exclusively on the Internet. This means that you are not location specific; you can have a really great lifestyle travelling and working at the same time. It's bliss when you know how!

Identify who your customers are. If what you're offering is business-to-business then you must have the following: a website, LinkedIn profile, Facebook page, Twitter account and definitely an email database. These online platforms are the absolute minimum to start out with. I advise using no more than three to four social media platforms because it can become a full-time job to just update them, look for content, and respond to interactions and comments. Set them up, have a plan and then make sure you monitor what happens when you post content, so you keep what works. Once you start making some money you can employ someone to help you with this. You may also need some productivity tools that will help you to do more in less time. Here are the ones that I use almost every day: Evernote, Hootsuite, Scrivener and Skype. I've written about them on my blog here www.unleashyourbusinessmojo.com/blogs.

You will also need to think about logos, flyers, business cards, and letterheads and cover photos for Facebook, LinkedIn and Twitter to give a consistent and familiar feel to your business. Make sure that you choose colours that stand out and are incorporated into all your printed materials and online platforms so that you become familiar to people. This is how you build a brand and position yourself in your industry. Places like Fiverr, PeoplePerHour and Upwork are great places to get people to do these things for you at a fraction of the high-street prices. Make sure you network like crazy. This is where you build on old relationships as well as create new ones. We'll talk more about networking later.

CHAPTER SEVEN

BRANDING

"If you're not branding yourself, you can be sure others will do it for you." ~ Unknown

To Niche or not to Niche…

As a business owner, you will also need to stand out and have your own niche[17]. A lot of new businesses are scared of niches, and I was too, because the fear is that you are locking out potential customers by defining the type of clients that you want to work with. The truth is that when you choose a target market you will be the expert for that target audience compared to someone who is just a generalist.

Find out what your target market want, and then give them what they need. It's the perfect way to sell because you may need to educate your audience about what they really need to get them to where they want to be.

---

[17] *Concentrating all marketing efforts on a small but specific and well defined segment of the population. Niches do not 'exist' but are 'created' by identifying needs, wants, and requirements of a particular market segment – www.businessdictionary.com (July 2016).*

Consider this scenario: you want to work with people who want to be millionaires. So you run a seminar entitled "Millionaires: How to Become One Now." People will rush to get on to the course when they see that headline. When they attend the seminar, you will then educate them on the type of person they need to become in order to be a millionaire - things like having the right mind-set, having a vision, writing down goals and working at them, not giving up no matter what, and being driven etc. It's about educating them on what it really takes. People want instant results, but not everyone has got what it takes to become a millionaire.

"Start by doing what's necessary; then do what's possible; and suddenly you are doing the impossible." ~ Francis Of Assisi[18]

Standing Apart

Standing out means having a great name, a great website, and a great message – plus a strapline that's memorable. Think about Tesco's "Every little helps" or "It's the real thing" by Coca Cola.

A purple cow - have you ever seen one? It's a metaphor used by the great Seth Godin, a thought leader in the area of sales and marketing. He says that your product or service should be like a purple cow, meaning that it should be very different from similar products. Even if it is an original product, a

---

[18] *Saint Francis of Assisi (Italian: San Francesco d'Assisi), born Giovanni di Pietro di Bernardone, informally named as Francesco (1181/1182 – 3 Oct. 1226), was an Italian Roman Catholic friar and preacher.*

common thing like a cow, you should make it purple so that it stands out. We've all seen original products give a modern or different twist to make them stand out. Dyson, iPads, George Foreman, Bosch speakers, Nike, Chromebooks, Phillips screwdrivers, Tippex, Ocado, Evian, McDonald's are a few of the products that have come into a crowded market but distinguished themselves as the proverbial "purple cow." A plain product transformed into an awesome new product through its packaging, size and colour, and consequently the price.

Taking this approach will help you stand out and get the publicity you need to grab people's attention, stimulate their curiosity, generate traffic, or whatever you need and want to make your business successful, i.e. more people buying from you.

When you start out you want to get a deeper understanding of your business and your customers, and therefore it follows that you should do your own marketing and get your hands dirty. It's better to do your own marketing yourself, especially at the beginning when there's no money and you probably don't know much about the different marketing routes. Don't hire a marketing consultant to do the work for you now; it's a waste of cash.

You still need to determine if your target audience is the right one. You need to know what they want. There are books, videos, and courses that can help you get more knowledge. Even if you do decide to take someone on in the future, this knowledge will prove valuable as you will be clearer about the skills and experience that your ideal employee will have to possess.

Don't start marketing too soon. Get your basics right first: your website and your social media profiles. What you don't want is people visiting them and not doing anything, or not knowing what to do when they get there, especially if you're paying for the traffic. You want to be sure that people are doing what you want them to do when they land on your website or other media channels - there must be a clear call to action.

Hello! Are you talking to me?

Make sure your message is targeted directly to the right audience - to do this, you need to know your potential buyers and the way they buy. There are persuasion techniques that you need to adopt to make sure that people actually buy from you, based on what you've said or written.

You need to romance your target audience. Also, check your content - use key words and make sure there are no grammatical errors. For organic traffic i.e. unpaid traffic you will need to do three things:

- Keyword – know the words your clients or target audience are using to search for your product or service and make sure you use these words on your website – Google

Keyword Planner is a free tool that can help you identify these keywords.

- Fresh content – make sure that your website is updated regularly, write blogs about what you offer, for instance if you're a holiday website have a blog about the best destinations holidays under £500. A plumber could write about how to fix a blocked drain
- Get others talking about you – business partners, suppliers, customers, with links to information that visitors to your website might need, a holiday website might have links to visas, home office advice & travel insurance
- Use Google Analytics to identify who, what and why the visitors are or aren't coming to your website. Why they are bouncing off, it will also tell you how long visitors to your website are staying, if its too short you might want to update or move your content around

Take advantage of the next big marketing tool – The mobile phone, over half of all internet searches now start on a mobile phone and 4 out of 5 of these consumers will call or go to that business within 24 hours. (Nectafy, 2014)

This means that when you're advertising your products or services on your website, you must make sure that you have your telephone number, address and good content on every page of your website, it seems obvious, but some businesses do forget these important points. If you don't make it easy for them to contact you – your competitors probably will.

Good Strategy = More traffic

Do have a smart strategy in place that drives traffic and also gets you paying customers. Make sure you are focusing on your target market. There's no point in promoting yourself to friends and family if they're not your target audience. Selling business-planning software to random people will not be as efficient as targeting those who are thinking of starting a business or fed up with working the 9-to-5 treadmill. You must be operating from a sales and marketing strategy that includes mini-campaigns, and these campaigns must be measured, managed and improved. Remember it's all about the benefits; no one buys anything based on features; people want to know how their lives or businesses will change by using your product or service.

Keep trying, change tack and strategy, but do not give up. You would not be reading this book if I had given up. Because, trust me, I had days when I wanted to jack it all in, but the only people who reap the benefits are those that follow through and get to the top of the ladder.

You must use your imagination to differentiate yourself and to borrow a quote from Napoleon Hill's[19] *Laws of Success*, Lesson 6:

""The products of your hands, minus imagination, will yield you but a small return, but those same hands, when properly guided by imagination, can be made to earn you all the material wealth you can use."

---

[19]   *Napoleon Hill (1883 – 1970) was an American author who became an early producer of personal-success literature. At the time of his death in 1970, his best-known work, Think and Grow Rich (1937) had sold more than 20 million copies, and over 70 million copies by 2011.*

So go forth and multiply - your wealth.

How to get customers

The first step to getting any customers these days is to create a sales funnel (*attracting as many potential customers as possible) to make sure you're getting the right people and keeping them interested right up to the buying stage.

First decide how you're going to sell to your clients. Since we're now in the digital age, there are very few things that can't be sold online. As mentioned earlier, you will need a website, social media channels, and hard copy promotional materials as well if you intend to do some networking offline.

What are you offering?

I'm in the information and service industry, so I offer my One Page Business Map as my value offer, and it's the first stage in my sales funnel.

Another thing that you need to be aware of is that you must have products that you can sell once the 'freebie' has been sent to visitors to your website. I understand you might be like me when I first started. For the first few times, I didn't even have a product. I just walked in to seminars and workshops and gave information on how to start a business; I was just so excited and happy to be in front of an audience, I didn't have my pricing and packages fine-tuned.   But then, as I was asked about my product, I created one - the One Page Business Map. And after that I created a 90-minute seminar around it.

I'm not sure if I gave too much away, but after the first few seminars I had very few people sign up for my higher priced products. I knew that I had to change the way I delivered the seminars. I needed to make it easier for people to buy my products. The obvious way was to sell my time, but that was just like having a job, and going straight from running seminars to one-to-one work was not ideal. I was selling myself too cheap – like a cheap date.

The best way is to sell digital informational products first, at a cheap price i.e. package your service, information, advice or training into a downloadable or online product. Then if customers need you they will have to pay more for a one to one meeting. This can be through a subscription-based system where they get to be coached by you once a month. If you have many customers, you can host a webinar where you address them as a group. This webinar can be recorded and given as a free product or sold to your customers.

Create Your Digital Products

If you're a consultant, think about what you're offering to potential and existing clients, and try to break them down into short courses. When you're making videos and audios, which I would advise you to do, make sure each video is no longer than five minutes – seven minutes at the most. Chunk it down, and make sure you have handouts to support what's on the videos or audios.

Scenario

If you're creating the first course it could consist of six modules broken down into five sections each, with each section lasting say five minutes. That's 25 minutes per section, multiplied by six modules, so that makes 150 minutes in total, which is two and a half hours. That's a reasonable length for a course. In the next course you can then go deeper into each section for those who need it. The first one will only be an introduction, and feedback from your customers will tell you where they need more help. You can then design courses around that.

"The entrepreneur always searches for change, responds to it, and exploits it as an opportunity."
~ Peter Drucker[20]

Once people have tried and liked your informational products, and want more, then it's time for them to meet you one-on-one at a higher price. This is where the money is made, and your time becomes worth more than it is now, while you're putting in less effort - because the products are sold online using an organised system, with your website and an online shop.

At each decision-making stage in the sales funnel, you want your clients to do something. This could be to like your

---

[20]   *Peter Ferdinand Drucker (1909 – 2005) was an Austrian-born American management consultant, educator, and author.*

Facebook page, watch a video, or sign up for your newsletter - whatever it is, you need to make it clear what it is you want them to do.

Packaging Your Products/Services

Think about what you're selling. How many products or services are you offering? You must have different packages and price levels that reflect the value of the product or service. If you're a web designer, for example, you could develop different packages covering: web development, logo and stationery design, SEO, content writing, hosting and web maintenance, domain registration, and social media set up and management.

If you're an accountant, you could have different packages for: payroll management, VAT returns, bookkeeping, sole trader accounts, company accounts, management accounting, or a combination of these.

Lawyers may offer help with conveyancing, immigration, civil litigation, wills, probate and inheritance tax, each as a separate package.

You get the picture. You need to make sure you bundle the packages so that they're attractive to the customer and meet their needs. If you're not sure, just research your competitors and see how they're packaging theirs. Then use that to come up with your own packaging and pricing options.

The Sales Funnel - My Steep Learning Curve

Yes, the sales funnel is a reality. It's the way you get more people to know about you and eventually buy from you. When I first started my business I did it the old fashioned way. I started in 2007, and my idea of advertising, as new businesses did back then, was to place an ad in the Yellow Pages and the Thomson directory. I registered with the local Chamber of Commerce and went to every networking event I heard about, whether it was relevant or not.

I was usually the lady with a bunch of business cards waiting to offload them to anyone I met, or in some cases forcing them upon my victims! I wasn't interested in what the people I met did; for one, I didn't have the confidence to ask them because I thought if they told me I'd probably have nothing much to say. So I didn't mix much, and I complained all the time about how no one called me out of the Yellow Pages blah blah blah. After revising my strategy, I decided to create the One Page Business Map and have now created seminars and online training programmes around it.

CHAPTER EIGHT

DIGITAL MARKETING

"Make it simple. Make it memorable.
Make it inviting to look at.
Make it fun to read."
~ Leo Burnett[21]

The rules for doing business have changed. Now you need to be online as well as offline. Almost everything is online now, and you need to be on specific channels depending on your target audience as well as your business location. There are so many platforms to choose from: websites, directories, social media, blogs, vlogs, with many more in the pipeline.

---

[21] *Leo Burnett (1891 – 1971) was an American advertising executive and the founder of Leo Burnett Company, Inc.*

This is a growing industry all of its own. It is already studied as a Master's degree - it's that important! What I get asked a lot is, "Which platform should I use?" Because no sooner have you chosen the ones that you want to focus on, another one crops up, or someone talks about how they've achieved success with the one you're not on! My advice is you might have to kiss a lot of frogs. For that reason, you have to tread carefully, and don't forget that this is your industry and you do have some Intel - yes, some business intelligence. Use that - because although you can rely on the advice of others, doing the work and testing what works best for your particular product or industry will be the best way forward.

If you don't have an online marketing presence, you are not going to be there to be found. And if you aren't there to be found, you're going to watch your business eventually disappear. You need to be online, and you need be online with a strategy in place.

You can have a beautiful website and an excellent business, but without search engine optimisation (SEO) you won't get very far - that's especially true for some businesses.

Social Media: The Facts

Social Media is where the money is, there are millions of potential customers waiting to buy your products or services. On social media they interact with brands and use it to decide what to buy, so it's important for your business to present on these platforms. According to Brandwatch, 72% of us trust online reviews and refer to at least one social media platform before we make a purchase. We now read blogs, testimonials and other reviews before we part with our cash.

The founders themselves have become the new 'rat pack' of social media, with many of them now multimillionaires, with even a few billionaires. Facebook enjoys a threesome with Instagram and more recently WhatsApp, for which it paid an eye-watering $22 billion. Even Snapchat's owner - the messaging/video platform popular with under 30s - is a billionaire at 25 years old!

Social media is good for your business because it can raise your website profile with Google, and ensure your website gets higher rankings when people search for the products or services that you offer. You can also pay for adverts on all of these platforms to grow your business faster, if done correctly.

So the main platforms are …

Facebook

Facebook is by far the most visited site, with over 1.65 billion members (2016). It is a great way to interact and keep in touch with both new and old customers.

However, do set up a Facebook page this is different from a

standard Facebook profile. It allows you to keep your Facebook profile private, so you can add on as many 'fans' as possible to your business by just getting them to like your page. If you do set up a business page try to post on it regularly, and keep your fans up to date with what you're doing. If you don't tell them they won't know!

Facebook is more suited to those who sell their products/services directly to the consumer. There are also paid adverts that appear that can produce good results. If you're advertising on Facebook, no other platform knows as much about you and your target customers. As of October 2014, over 70% of new business contacts first heard about each other on Facebook.

Here is a tip for posting on Facebook. Try to post half an hour before work begins or after lunchtime, research has shown that these times see a higher number of views.

Twitter

Another big one is Twitter, with over 320 active million users (2016) generating more than 500m tweets a day. Personally, I don't use this site as much as I would like to, but for those who use it properly it does seem to work for them. It allows you to send up to 140 characters in one tweet, and you can tag others in your tweet. There is a hashtag, which is used to organise tweets so that others can search for them more easily. I have met people in my network who have over 16k followers. The advantages of using Twitter are that it is very personal and responses are quick, so you need to have the resources to reply to tweets. You will lose trust if you don't. There are followers, tweets, and retweets that you need to manage. Always ask the question, "Why am I tweeting?" Remember to be careful about what you tweet too - you can delete the tweet but not the heat! Kenneth Cole and Paddy Power are two infamous twitter handlers.

LinkedIn

LinkedIn is very good for professionals and businesses that offer products and services to other professionals and businesses. It's easy to set up a profile - be sure to add a photo, some testimonials, and include links to your website.

Joining different forums on LinkedIn and posting comments about your business expertise is a great way to get known. LinkedIn has over 400 million users in nearly 200 countries. There is a paid version, but the free one is adequate for most users. It's great for acquiring new leads and the best platform of the lot for business-to-business contact. However, you must know your audience. Being an accountant and joining many accountancy forums and groups is not ideal. By all means join a few, but make sure that you join groups that reflect your target audience.

Do have a profile picture that is clear and shows you in a professional light. Give value and post good content, remembering to engage and ask questions. Be prepared to monitor your results too. Who's viewing your profile? What do they do? Write blogs, and then check to see how many people are reading them and how many like them. What do you think your target audience might want to read about? Go and write about that!

Instagram/Pinterest

Now, if you're in the design, fashion or food industry Pinterest is like gold dust for your business, because you can post your pictures and get them liked - or 'pinned' i.e. shared with other people. Your name and product can spread like wildfire. It is popular with women and the busiest times being between 8 to 11 pm on Saturday.

Be sure to tag your website in your pictures so that you get clicks back to your website. This is all very important for your search engine optimisation.

Instagram is similar to Pinterest in that it's a picture-sharing platform. It's used by the big brands too, to keep their brand alive, generate interest, and enter new markets. You can also post short videos on it. Apparently, pizza is the most popular instagrammed food.

YouTube

YouTube is getting bigger. Since Google owns it, web searches also bring up YouTube videos. It's the second largest search engine after Google, with over one billion users.

When you are posting a video on YouTube, do make sure that you select the right category. Do your 'About Us' and profile page with the channel cover, and make sure that you put up your website link so that visitors can see it there.

You don't need to be a video director to create and upload a video. All you need to get started is your mobile phone and a bit of motivation. Make sure you have good content, a purpose, and an engaging topic. And if you get stuck for ideas, just ask your target audience what their problems/challenges are, and create a video addressing just one of those problems. When they start commenting, you can respond to their questions, or even ask them directly what they want you to talk about next.

Have a theme to your videos to get people coming back to watch you. Whatever you decide to do - be consistent. YouTube, like so many blogs, has channels that have only ever had one video posted on them - and then it's added to the heap of 'coulda' beens.'

The famous YouTubers do it all day long, and these are the new Internet millionaires - all from vlogging about what their viewers want to see. Keep your video short though. Although some do go on for about 16-20 minutes, even 2 hours, my suggestion though, would be three to four minutes, and six minutes as an absolute maximum. Make sure you share your videos on blogs, websites, and other platforms.

WhatsApp

WhatsApp is not quite a social media platform, but it is a great communication tool and can be used to send messages and updates to your contacts via their telephone numbers. It also allows you to set up groups, and I've used it to put together small coaching groups for my clients. It's more interactive and because it's a mobile phone based platform, people are more likely to see the messages you post. It has amassed over 900 million users worldwide.

Of course, there are other platforms, but these are the main ones. Not all platforms will work for you.

Some people swear by Twitter and LinkedIn, others love YouTube, and some think Facebook is where it happens! My suggestion is to have a profile in at least three/four places, and spend time trying to get familiar with them and seeing which channels work for your business. Since it's about business, it's the one that you get more traction from that you'll have to stick with. Do your research - test, measure and see what works best for your business. As time goes on, when you understand the media channels that bring the best results, you can get someone to work on these social media channels for you so that you can spend more time on your business and attracting more customers. Some people do have a business that just operates on social media; however, you also need...

CHAPTER NINE

YOUR WEBSITE

"Websites promote you 24/7:
No employee will do that."
~ Paul Cookson[22]

The website should cater for your target audience. It should engage visitors so that they stay long enough to provide their email address or buy something. To achieve this, you need to offer them something to make them leave their email address - it must be something of value to them.

So, say you're an accountant. Your website could allow visitors to download the White Paper on the new tax savings, give information on ways to save tax or pay less tax on their property, or offer them a free diagnostic for their business.

---

[22] *Paul Cookson, British author and poet (born 1961)*

If you're an estate agent it could be a free listing of their property on your website, advice on how to improve their property so that it sells in less than a month, or ten ways to increase their property price by £10,000.

A business consultant could offer business owners a guide on how to double their email list in seven days, a free review of their website, or a list of seven blog headlines that will ensure their emails are opened.

There are other ways of making offers, such as compiling a video series, e-books, webinars and newsletters. You could give potential customers your offer via your website, as well as through other channels, such as social media, networking in person, and when you speak at events.

Take a leaf out of the book of the bigger retailers, which offer you a discount on your first purchase. Waitrose, Next, Clarks, Debenhams and Tesco are a few that do that - in return they get your email address, and then use it to sell even more to you.

Your website must be optimised, i.e. be designed to attract the right visitors to each page. You must also make visitors stay long enough to do what it is you want them to do. Each page can actually be targeted at a different product or service. For example, an accountant can target each page at a particular service they offer for example, one for personal tax and another page for business tax so that visitors are engaged when they're on that page.

Also, different items can be added to each page to ensure that Google optimises the page. I'm sure you've heard about algorithms. This is how Google decides what's important, and why your page needs to be listed in the search engine or ranked so that it comes up when a topic related to your subject area is mentioned. Keywords used on your website should match the keywords that your target audience will be searching for, and when they get there it should have enough information to make them want to stay. Your free offer must also be relevant to them and be compelling enough for them to leave their email address. Your website should be linked up to a customer relationship manager/database, so that when they drop in their email address the item is sent to them and they are added to your database. If it is organised properly you will know how, why, and where someone gave you their email address. I use MailChimp. So, what's the best way to get a website? You might want to consider these options for getting...

The Best Website You Can Afford

When I was going to launch my new business website, I explored many options and there are many. First, there are those that I call "web in a box". They have various templates that you can choose from, and you just cut and paste in your information and pictures - and hey presto, your website is ready. Moonfruit, Wix and Vistaprint are the forerunners in this arena. Prices start at about £60 per year. Whatever you do, don't get the free versions because they look very unprofessional with their logos emblazoned across your website.

Then there are the ones that you build yourself - from scratch: WordPress, Jumia, and the lesser known Drupal fall into this category. Their web builder software relies on plug-ins, widgets and add-ons, which you have to download - similar to the apps on smartphones. They're mostly free; although there are some with premium features that you have to pay for. You will also need a host and someone to update the site.

The final option is to pay someone to take the pain away and deliver your shiny new website to you. This costs anything from £400, plus update costs.

Website in a Box

I tried this one a few years ago and I didn't like the 'web-in-a-box' websites because they weren't as flexible as I wanted them to be. They had set templates, so you ended up with a 'me too' website, and I had also read about some of them not being responsive - a term used to describe the way a website is scalable so that it's easy to view on mobile devices. Another reason I didn't like them was because it can be hard to manage and monitor your Search Engine Optimisation (SEO).

D.I.Y Websites?

After reflecting on the options, I decided to build my first website myself, from scratch, using WordPress templates. I didn't know anything about website designs, html codes,

PHPs, plug-ins, add-ons, themes and widgets etc. But with Dr Google and a couple of very good YouTube videos, I was able to build a basic website that made some people go WOW! Impressed that I built it with no experience - yes? You probably are - but it cost me a lot of blood, sweat and tears! However, I now had a virtual place where my potential clients and customers could visit me, read about me, and get their MOJO back.

Will I build another website again? If I can afford not to, I won't. It took longer than I thought. I gave up in frustration many times and missed my deadline by three weeks, but a limited budget and a looming deadline are great motivators, so I forged ahead. It was a great experience, and it made me think about my business in more detail. Because I'd built my website on WordPress I could go in and change things around, adding and taking away information without having to pay and rely on a web developer, with those secret PHP, admin and html codes. A good website needs constant tweaking, and Google will reward your hard work by ranking you much better than if you just left it with no changes at all. When people ask me which option they should go for – I tell them, "If you have the time and PATIENCE go ahead and do it yourself. If you can afford to, get someone else to do it!" No matter what you decide, make sure you buy and register your own domain - website name. If you do pay someone to build your website, remember you will still have to provide them with all the content (information) that you want on your website, and you'll also have to guide them towards how you want it to look, the colours, layout, number of pages etc.

My current website was built for me by a designer I found on PeoplePerHour, after trying out at least six designers and with lots of tears and frustration. This was because my original website was down for nearly six weeks - the one I built myself got hacked! Do make sure you get your website backed up regularly.

Now that you have a website, it's time to think about...

Getting Traffic to Your Website

Your website, when it is newly formed, will not have traffic. You are new, so no one knows about you or your business - just yet. A few friends might visit. Some people you hand your business card to might also visit out of curiosity, but the bottom line is that very few people will know where you are, so you need to use other forums and seek creative ways to get traffic to your website. So look at ways you can position yourself and your business; seek and get involved with relevant larger platforms where you can engage with your target audience.

Growing your own site organically will take time and slow down your growth - do a combination of both to ensure early success. Other platforms like Facebook, Twitter, Amazon and

Etsy all perform different functions, but the key thing they do is bring traffic. You may be able to benefit from that traffic if your sales funnel is set up in such a way that it engages your target audience.

For example, Etsy is for home furnishing, crafts and bespoke fashion. So if you're setting up as a fashion designer I would advise you to set up there because it already has the traffic. And if you were selling a nice custom-made dress then that would be the place for you. Of course, you'll have a link to your website listed there as well.

Large stores also understand and appreciate the need to be on other platforms. Office Shoes in the UK is a big fashion chain specialising in shoes. It has over 150 physical stores and an online presence; yet it has a shop on eBay and Amazon too. This just demonstrates the need to be where your customers are to make sure that you get that sale. Debenhams, one of the UK's biggest department stores, is also on Amazon. So you get the picture. Use other platforms to leverage your business.

Paying For Traffic

You might be wondering how people will find out about your website. This is where you might need to spend money. Facebook ads are great for this because you can spend a few pounds a day to boost the visits to your website by getting Facebook to run ads that place you in front of your target audience. They do this successfully. I have been targeted this way, and it worked. I ended up buying a course about how to sell on Facebook, which is why I'm able to show you how it's done.

YouTube is another great place to advertise. When people in your target market are searching for something to help them, you can place your advert on the video that relates to their problem or need. For example, if you coach young people going to university you might want to target the videos that they watch, such as videos on how to study. If you sell make-up products you might want to advertise on a 'how to' make-up video. If you sell shoes then target videos about OOTD – which stands for 'outfit of the day' in YouTube land.

You can also make more money by becoming an affiliate for any product that you demonstrate or are talking about. If you're talking about someone else's product, or a company's product or service, and they don't already have an affiliate programme, make sure that you ask for a discount for recommending them to your readers, viewers, or anybody who ends up buying the product because of you. It's called product placement, affiliate marketing, or celebrity endorsement, and it's just a way of making more money.

Website – Hacks and Tips

In web design, there's the F-layout, which suggests that when we visit a website we tend to focus on the left-hand side, and our eye movements on a website mirrors the letter F.

This means that your opt-in box might do better being on the left, rather than on the right which is the go-to place for most websites. It also follows that relevant blogs or articles are also on the left-hand side, and things like contact and other blog posts are on the right. The opt-in box should also be above the fold to ensure that as visitors land on the page they don't need to scroll down to see the box. Some websites actually place the opt-in box at the top of the page.

Why It's Good to Blog Yourself to Fame and Success

Another great way to market online is to write about your product or service and this is also known as blogging. It can generate quite a bit of interest and will also help your website with Google rankings as long as the content is relevant and fresh – updated periodically.

Blogging is massive. There are now over 170 million blogs available, and the two most popular platforms are Word Press and Blogger.

However, a large majority of these blogs are not regularly updated. Many start off well and within a few weeks are forgotten, never to add another post. I have been on both sides of the fence. I started a blog with every intention of following through, making it a top destination for my readers, and climbing up the Google rankings. Unfortunately, procrastination coupled with my spirit of perfectionism killed my budding dream before I could even load my first entry. I stumbled at the 'About Me' page, trying to aim for the perfect content to put there and just gave up!

The other time, I took up roller-skating so went online looking for inspiration and I started to follow a lady who had also just taken up roller-skating, but was further ahead than I was. She wrote a couple of entries and then just stopped writing with no warning. I enjoyed it so much I kept going back for weeks, hoping and expecting her to return. She never did. Both blogs were committed to the 'bloggers graveyard', forever!

'Happily for me, I've moved on and rekindled my blogging dream. I started over again.

But back to the question: Why blog for business?

"Either write something worth reading or do something worth writing."
~ Benjamin Franklin

Research has shown that blogging is a great way to get people to know about what you do, and it helps to promote your business. You become known as an expert in your industry, especially if you decide to keep your blog limited to a specific topic or area. Google also loves bloggers, because it means your content is fresh and you are active which drives traffic to your website or blog. Google rewards you by listing your blog in the top searches that relate to your blog content, based on keywords.

For me, it's about reading a lot more, and getting into the habit of writing something useful every week, something that will be a resource for my readers, clients, and possibly a book. Top bloggers also rake in the pennies, with some earning over $2 million per year, while others earn that in just a month! - *The Huffington Post* apparently does. And its not just about making money monthly, it's also about building a BUSINESS that can be sold. 22-year-old John Wu did just that when he sold his blog for an eye- popping $15 million.

MOJO Hacks:

- Read more, don't aim for perfection, know that you will get better with time, ask your clients and target audience what their challenges are and write about that
- Your goal is to communicate what they want and need, and also to get them to take action
- Keep it simple – there's no need to show off your grammatical prowess by writing 20 words where three will do. Time is valuable for all of us, and if people do decide to read your blog, make it as pleasurable as possible for them, so they keep coming back

---
CHAPTER TEN

NETWORKING

*"I've learned that people will forget
what you said, people will forget
what you did, but people will never
forget how you made them feel."*
~ Maya Angelou[23]

A s well as social media and websites, there are some marketing avenues that are traditional and still work for some industries. I will name a few and give examples of the products or services that it's best to use these routes for.

Your product or service does not bring people to you. Your advertising and marketing does that, so you need to build that into your marketing strategy - this is the one thing you must do all the time. Marketing brings customers to the business,

---

[23]   *Maya Angelou, born Marguerite Annie Johnson (1928 – 2014) was an American poet, memoirist, and civil rights activist.*

customers bring money, and money gives you the freedom and the opportunity to fulfil your dreams.

Offline marketing is basically about building relationships to ensure that your business is foremost in the minds of your potential customers as well as your existing ones.

The Elevator Pitch

The first tool in your armoury is how you introduce your business – Your elevator pitch.

As I've mentioned before, one of the easiest ways to grow your business is through networking. This is when you attend events, where you meet other business owners and potential clients. You will have to introduce yourself and explain what you do and how your service or product can help them. It's a great way to sell yourself in person and to make great contacts for potential business, career development, and future referrals. However, when you attend these events you have just a few seconds to make the right impact with your introduction - which is normally called an 'elevator pitch'.

It's called an elevator pitch because you should be able to explain what you do in the time it takes for a lift to move from one floor to the next - less than 30 seconds!

Picture this: you're dressed the part, you have a pocket full of business cards, and you're in a room full of like-minded entrepreneurs - the gateway to more customers and potential referrals. The icing on the cake is to be able to introduce yourself with clarity and passion, conveying the benefits of your product or service, and keeping it short all at the same time.

How do you do that? With practice. There are three things to note about your elevator pitch:

- It must be short
- You must say it with enthusiasm
- And it must convey the benefits or value to the listener

I use the miniskirt analogy to demonstrate this: It must be long enough to cover the important parts, but short enough to arouse interest.

Identifying the benefits of your product and service is not as easy as it seems. I often go to events where people talk more about the features of their business (product or service) than the benefits - even I'm guilty of doing this sometimes. It's a bit like selling the sizzle of the bacon and not the bacon itself. Try watching some adverts, especially ones for perfume. Notice that there's rarely ever any mention of the ingredients; it's about what the product can do for you. So if you're a male, you get all the girls chasing you. And if you're a girl, you become irresistible and sexy. And we buy into that dream.

When you've finished delivering your elevator pitch, you want people fawning all over you! Okay, maybe that's a bit much, but you are hoping to be asked, "How do you do that?" or "Tell me more."

> Task: Practice doing your elevator pitch in front of a mirror, and record it on your smartphone. Practise until you're able to deliver it in 30 seconds, making sure you mention the BENEFITS, not features.

Do you need help crafting your elevator pitch? I can help you with that.

The Business Card

The next tool in your armoury is your business card - you must have some with you at all times. Use a pen or make a mental note of the conversations you have so that it's easier to remember, after the meeting. These days, with mobile phones you can actually store these contacts in different ways, including apps that can take photos of the business card and transfer the contact details directly onto a database, saving you tons of time.

Be interested in other people - you really don't know how much you might have in common with them. Do ask them what they do and their name, and perhaps why they've come along to the meeting or event you're at. And then, when they ask you about yourself, feel free to talk about the benefits of what you do. Trust me, some people don't ask and are just happy to keep on talking. Don't worry; listen for as long as you can. Judge the situation and try to steer the conversation away from them, or just walk away politely, pretending you want to visit the restroom.

You can also team up with someone who has the same target audience as you and ask to share their database. It may be at a cost, but it will be more productive and more rewarding than cold calling - or trying to find all your customers yourself.

Hosting Events

Hosting events is another way to get other people interested in what you do. Being the speaker is great because you are the centre of attention, and the audience will ask questions and see you as the expert. People in the audience might also recommend you to their own network or to other useful business contacts that could help you down the line. I use this system and have built my database by presenting and hosting events, alone and with others. Going it alone can be difficult, because you will have to be the one to find the clients, present the material, organise refreshments and a venue, and you will also have to sell to them.

If you don't host events, you can find events to attend. People run events across London every day, and many of them are looking for speakers. Just go on to the Eventbrite website and search for the kind of events that would attract the kind of clients that you would like to reach and contact the organiser asking for an opportunity to speak at the event. I host a free monthly women's networking event in my area – a venture, which came about from meeting the founder of NELE at another networking event.

Printed Media

Newspapers have been around longer than any other form of printed media and are the go-to advertising resource for many small businesses. People aged over 45 years are more likely to read things in print, so they are the ones to target when using newspaper advertising. Newspapers are good for marketing offers and for selling services to local audiences, like motorcar repairs, plumbers, gardeners, property and legal services.

Flyers

Flyers are also a popular way of marketing, so let's cover a few important points about using a flyer. Make sure you highlight the benefits of your service or product on your flyer - not the features! Be clear whether you want potential customers to call, download a file, book a free session, or get a discount - make sure the 'call to action' is very clear.

If you decide to give out the flyers you need to make sure that you're in the right location, with the right target audience. For example, if it's a beauty product that you're promoting then you will need to be in a location that is frequented by women who use such beauty products.

Look at the return on investment, and include the cost of designing, printing and distributing the leaflet so that you can measure the effectiveness of the flyer.

Some businesses can also benefit from door-to-door marketing. You can use local newspapers that will insert your flyers into the paper, or just hire some people to drop leaflets door to door. For example, this works well for takeaway restaurants, MOT and motor garages, estate and letting agents, loan providers and home improvement services. Identify the area very well though; if you're selling double-glazing there will be no point in giving out flyers in an area where residents who do not own their own homes.

There are three simple things that you should also include in your marketing strategy that do not cost any money:
• Always ask for referrals from your existing customers
• Always ask for testimonials
• Have a keep-in-touch strategy - email marketing helps to ensure that your customers remember you

And put some of these testimonials on all your promotional material - including your online portals.

Joint Ventures

You can team up with people who offer goods or services to people in a similar target market, where those services or products complement yours. For example, if you are a wedding photographer you can team up with someone who makes cakes or decorates the hall, even a wedding dress designer or a car hire provider. You get the picture? Offer discounts to customers; this will encourage them to buy more.

CHAPTER ELEVEN

EMAIL MARKETING

"Advertising is the literature of desire."
~ Eugene M Schwartz[24]

Be Visible to your herd

Coca Cola is one of the world's most recognised brands, yet it still spends over $3.5 billion on advertising every year. But if you haven't got their budget, networking could help you.

Here, I give you the skinny on networking. Love it or hate it, it's a great way to grow your business, and it costs very little. You can network online or by physically attending events.

Did you know that we let at least 80 per cent of our potential clients fall through the cracks? How? By not following up after an event (seminars, exhibitions, networking events, first enquires). Yes, according to research, people do not follow up

---

[24] *Eugene M Schwartz (1927– 1995) was an American author and copywriter.*

on potentially hot business leads! That is lost time and money.

I can testify to this. When I attend events and take someone's card, I will send an email to them or connect with them some other way. But I have found that of those I send an email to, less than half respond, even after I send them a second email. How many times has someone tried to sell you something, and although you've been keen they've never got back in touch with you? See, they missed a sale! How much money are you leaving on the table by not following up on your own warm leads?

Most of our new business/customers will actually come from people we don't know very well. Research has shown that most of the people we know have the same resources and probably belong to the same networks that we do, so we have to look beyond our current networks and approach people in new networks. This can open us up to a whole new set of people, resources and opportunities.

I understand that we're all busy, and some of the typical excuses I come across are:
- I don't have time to network because I'm so busy with my current customers/clients
- I don't know how to network – I'm too shy and don't want to sound like a used car salesman

But, if you haven't got a sales team, you are the sales team.

Focus on building relationships. Remember that phrase: people buy from people they like. Become likeable. Show that you're interested in others. Steve Covey in his book "*7 Habits of Highly Successful People*" says, "*Seek first to understand, then be understood.*" Everyone loves talking about themselves, so ask people you meet about themselves and their business.

For those who are interested in your services, follow up – immediately! With other new leads keep in touch by sending them information that might help them. For instance, you may want to tell them about other suitable networking / training events that might benefit them, or you could send them a link to an article that might interest them. If you have a database put them on it, so they remember you – each time you send an email and they will buy from you when they are ready and you have something that they have.

Whilst the people you meet at some events may not need your product or services, they may know someone who does. Some deals will be as a result of the most unlikely contacts and come at the most unexpected time.

So you've made the contacts. What next?

Keeping in Touch with Contacts

As the online marketers parrot, "Your money is in your list." So you need to start building yours, because when you have about 5,000 contacts - which seems to be the magical number - you can start using it to leverage more sales and customers. Think of all the emails you get from companies trying to sell you more things - and do the same.

Here are five tips to take you to the top 20% of successful networkers who follow up! (It's definitely lonely at the top!)

- Decide on a system to keep all your contacts in one place. A spreadsheet used to be the only option, but now there are so many online CRMs out there, such as MailChimp - I use this and it's free if you send fewer than 12,000 emails a month and have no more than 2,000 email contacts

- Decide on the number of events you want to attend if you're going to start following up on them because it can be quite time-consuming. I would suggest no more than two events a week. If you meet six people it could take up to an hour to craft and send out a personalised email. This time will shorten as you become a pro at writing follow-up emails after networking events

- Remember that when you go to networking events, giving out your card is not a priority, because we now know that very few people follow up anyway. Getting cards is a must though, and do try to find out more about the person so that, when you go to Tip 5 below, you have something specific to write about

- In this era of social media, be sure to get details of people's LinkedIn, Twitter and Facebook accounts. I know a lady who takes her tablet with her and adds people to her social media pages on the spot - a great time saver!

- Send follow-up emails after an event. I have scoured my sent email box, and here are a few samples that you can adapt.

Sample 1

"As promised, here is the xxxxx that I have recently developed as part of my coaching tools. You can use it to help flesh out your ideas and vision for your business. It can be filled in on your PC, so there is no need to print it out.

I hope you find it useful. Do let me know how you get on with it."

Sample 2

"It was nice meeting you last night. Thanks for keeping us topped up with drinks and ensuring the food area did not become chaotic. I am just touching base with you to find out more about what you do, as we didn't have much time to talk last night. I am a business coach and work mainly with women, and I would love to know more about your events in xxxx."

Sample 3

"It was nice to meet you on Saturday at xxx's event. Hope you had as much fun as I did. I It was great meeting so many phenomenal women from such diverse backgrounds.

I would also be grateful if you could send me the contact details of the lovely 'xxxxx' lady who had a stall next to you, as I seem to have misplaced her details.

Do take care, and be sure to add me to your mailing list."

Now you are armed with some networking skills and tips to grow your business. Get out there! Get networking! And remember to stay in touch!

MOJO Hacks:
- Go to Eventbrite, and choose three events that you think might help to grow your business or your network. Attend these events and make contact with at least three people. Get to know them, and keep in touch
- Use MailChimp or AWeber for setting up a database and keeping in touch

---

CHAPTER TWELVE

POWER IN BUSINESS

'Impossible is just a big word thrown around by small men who find it easier to live in the world they've been given than to explore the power they have to change it. Impossible is not a fact. It's an opinion. Impossible is not a declaration. It's a dare. Impossible is potential. Impossible is temporary. Impossible is nothing.'
~ Muhammad Ali

By power in business I don't mean the power to take over the world (well you can if you want to), but the ability to create a better outcome for your business or "to make things happen" as defined by the business dictionary. While some may see power as bad, please ignore that viewpoint. Consider all that you have been told about power - that it's unpleasant. Really? Well if you want to be successful in business you really need to get some power and I will share with you why you need power and what you need to do to get it.

Why Having Power is a Good Thing

You have to stand out and be different. Being at the top is for a few people only, and if you want to be one of them you need to make sure you brand yourself differently from everyone else. You need to play to win. It's not a fair or just world - games are played, politics exist well beyond the political realms, and to say you are not political is like saying you don't breathe. What I am asking you to do is to accept this and then understand how it works, so that you have a better chance of winning.

Let's get personal: your business should stand out and be memorable. Even if you are going into an industry that is populated with others, you can still stand out. There are very few new things, and people have succeeded in becoming leaders in competitive markets. Super Jam's founder was 14 years old when he started his international brand of jams. Every supermarket has its own brand of jam, in addition to all the other well-known brands like Hartley's and Robertson's; yet he still went into this highly competitive market and has done very well. His secret to success is his ability to keep going. Waitrose rejected him because they didn't like his original packaging. He's also not afraid to ask for help - the Innocent drinks founder helped him with packaging. He is now stocked in most retailers in the UK and has expanded the brand to other countries.

Feeling Uncomfortable about being Powerful?

Like it or not, people who promote themselves and brag about it are more likely to get what they want, and you have to start getting comfortable with doing just that. Stop worrying about what others think of you. To be honest, they're too worried about how they look and how they come across to others!

Yes, powerful people are often seen as bad, and because of this we don't try hard enough to get and use our own power. Another reason is that a lot of us are afraid of failing, so we don't go out of our way to pursue what we need to become more powerful.

One of the biggest mistakes that you can make is to think that intelligence wins hands down. It doesn't - and research has shown that the most intelligent and the most knowledgeable people do not get the promotions or the contracts. Actually, it's the ones that know how to court those in power, or know how to use their power to get what they want and need, that win all the time.

Do you know that most people do not ask for the help they need because of their fear of rejection? Some of the people with the knowledge or resources that you want will be flattered to share that information with you, as long as you ask them in a nice way or flatter them -- *"Be my mentor"* or *"Who do you know that builds websites?"* Notice that I said, *"Who do you know?"* Not, *"Do you know anyone?"* As humans, we're lazy, so if given a chance we will go for the easiest answer, and the answer to the second question is a simple no or yes. Whereas the first question forces you to think of someone that you do know that can build websites. A slight change, but it can make the difference between getting what you want or not.

Look at the people around you. Are they on the same journey as you are, or do they represent where you want to go? If they're not, then you need to start aligning yourself with people that can take you to where you want to go, or who are already where you want to be.

You're no more than six people away from that person you need to meet.

Identify the movers and shakers within your industry. Get close to them. You need to be visible, and it's in your interests for you to be known. Build a reputation so that when you're introduced to someone or your name is mentioned people have heard of you, somehow or somewhere. You need to make sure that those that have the power remember you. Power is like the Pareto principle - the 80:20 rule: 20% of power is given, while the other 80% you will have to take. So start getting used to blowing your own trumpet, because no one else will do it for you.

Why You Need Power

Working in a team doesn't have to be your reality. Leaders and people with power occupy positions on their own: presidents, CEOs, governors, permanent secretaries, keynote speakers, lead coaches and monarchs. Some species - the honeybee colony for example - even go to extremes. When the queen bee hatches the first thing she does is destroy all the other queen bees that are yet to hatch, and if for some reason the queen bees happen to hatch at the same time they will all fight till death, until only one remains. Even in small groups when tasks are given out, where the task giver identifies no leader, the group will choose a leader.

In his book *Power: Why Some People Have It - and Others Don't*, Jeffery Pfeffer[25] explains that we should learn the rules of the game and apply them to be successful, and to do what is necessary to get ahead. Concentrate on self-knowledge, building confidence, and being tolerant. Forget about whether you like the person that you need to get close to; make sure not liking a person isn't the reason you're holding back your career or business.

Be ready to stand out and be recognised - that's the rule of advertising. A lot of big brands don't advertise to make us buy

25   *Jeffrey Pfeffer (born 1946, Missouri), is an American business theorist and the Thomas D. Dee II Professor of Organizational Behaviour at the Graduate School of Business, Stanford University, and is considered one of today's most influential management thinkers.*

their products or services, but rather to remind us that they're there, so that when we do decide to buy we choose them because they're familiar. Become familiar and recognised amongst your target audience. People must know about you and feel comfortable with you.

Weak ties are actually your strongest links. Close friends and family have access to the same networks as you do, but those weak links can introduce you to new networks and can grow your business.

CHAPTER THIRTEEN

SOME TECHNICALITIES ...

The Legal side to setting up your own Business

Starting up in business also has legal and tax implications, which you must be aware of to make sure you don't end up in trouble. Do make sure that you get advice early on. People pay huge fines for non-compliance, so be careful and don't assume anything. As a new business owner there are some things that you will need to have in place - start building your company as you mean to go on. Having the right policies and procedures, registering with the right agencies, having the right insurance and licences in place are all part of what you will need to do - and exactly what you need to do will depend on your industry.

Below are some of the types of business structures that you could choose, with the key things to consider.

Flying Solo

You can start up as self-employed, which is the simplest form of self-employment. You can choose any name (which could be yours) and start trading straightaway. Just remember to register with your tax office, depending on your location and country.

With Company

You are distinct from the business and may want the cloak of limited liability. If that's the case, the other option is to set up a limited company. You will be the director of this company and will have to register with Companies House via their website, if you're based in the UK.

This option does require more thought. You can buy off-the-shelf companies or set one up yourself. Do bear in mind that each type of set-up has its own set of requirements in terms of reporting. For instance, as a limited company you will have to prepare annual accounts for both the HMRC and Companies House at specific times, and there are penalties for late submissions. With the self- employed option there are fewer returns to submit, but there are still penalties for late submissions. Do seek help from an accountant or tax adviser to ensure that you start with the best advice. I have come across many business owners who could have benefitted from getting the right advice at the right time. Get proper advice: tax rules and tax laws change all the time, so please do not wing this one.

Other set-ups are where you are in a relationship with another person, company or others and can take the form of:

- CIC companies for the community - where profits/surpluses are reinvested back into the company, and
- LLPs - which are mainly for lawyers and accountants and have different rules governing them.
- But do get some professional advice first.

Now you need to consider...

Where to pitch your tent

Should you rent an office or work from home? This is the 64-million-dollar question. Let's look at some of the things to consider.

There are so many variables, but cash plays a major role. Other considerations are: the type of business you're developing, your target customers, geographical location and how you want to position yourself and your business.

In the service industry, with consultants, insurance brokers and travel agents, it's easier for businesses to start up with no physical office address - just a spare room, or even a corner of a bedroom will do just fine. The basic requirements are a smartphone, laptop, printer and stationery.

You could also consider a virtual office address. Some may not allow you to meet clients at their location, but they will give you the opportunity of putting their address on your business stationery and website. For an extra fee you may get access to a small meeting room that you can use when you have appointments with your clients. Or just use coffee shops and hotel lobbies - I did that in the beginning.

In the retail business, if you're selling fashion goods online you can get away with having an online shop, instead of a physical shop, but you may still need a physical address for returns and your supplier's deliveries. Having an address will also give people confidence to shop with you – although, if you use portals like Amazon, they can do all that for you - at a price. Yes, you basically have your products delivered to them, and they stock and sell them – it's called Fulfilled By Amazon.

A physical office address might also help in some instances, depending on the image that you want your business to project. Some businesses, like estate agents and hairdressers, may also want to attract passing trade so may need office space. .

Using your home

It's much cheaper. And you can avoid the stress of the daily commute and of dodging smelly armpits! - Thus saving you time and travel costs, and giving you some fresh air. You can also have whatever you want for lunch - without the price tag! On the flip side, it can be less productive. If I don't have an action plan or some written goals/objectives to meet, then it becomes a bit difficult to get motivated. Sometimes, speed and quality are sacrificed when we work from home. It can also be a challenge to meet clients if you don't want to bring them into your house, and meeting at Starbucks or in a hotel lobby is not always ideal for some clients.

Working alone can also be boring. This is supported by recent studies which reveal that the number of people who don't have someone to bounce ideas off or discuss important issues with has tripled over the last two decades, which leads to reduced productivity and profits.

Working from an office

Working away from home means there are clear working boundaries and fewer distractions, such as the TV, the fridge, and even the thought of taking a quick nap. Although working in an office can create the impromptu "water fountain meetings," paying for office space can force you to focus on putting more effort into your business and consequently you're likely to be more productive and your business more profitable.

The main disadvantage here is the cost of paying for office space and the associated costs of travel and the extra resources required.

Some businesses do have to operate from an office, no matter how small they are. Would you trust a lawyer or doctor with no office premises? Your decision should be based on the type of business model you have and whether you will need regular contact with your customers/clients.

Are you self-motivated? If you're easily distracted, you might benefit from having the structured working environment that a rented office can offer. Finally, do you like working alone or do you prefer having people around you? Assess the cost/benefit of each option, and this will help you to choose the one that suits you and your business.

Hiring Your First Virtual Assistant (VA)

There comes a time in your business when you realise that you need help and that you will have to delegate those mundane tasks that remain so long on your to-do list. When you begin to dread looking at them, that's the time to call in the listbusters – your very own virtual assistant (VA). One area of business management that I find my clients have challenges with is their social media. You can't be everywhere at once, and managing a business and having to update your statuses online can take time and effort.

Some of the things that I get my VA to do, that you may need help, with include:

- Doing online research and creating content for blogs
- Updating databases, tagging records, and organising lists on my CRM
- Updating my website

The key things for a smoother journey are to interview them first, and make sure that you try out at least two - don't expect miracles. The first one you employ may not be the best, but at under $5 per hour, you can afford some risks.

Obviously, to get the most out of your VA, make sure you have a list of things that they can do on a weekly basis, say four hours a week to start off with. Be willing to train them and show them exactly how you want each task to be completed. It's not a "delegate and forget" scenario. It's still your business, so you need to be on top of things and make sure you get daily check-ins/updates.

To find someone suitable:
- Register and search for suitable candidates. VAs from the Philippines are best for admin, while those from the Far East and Eastern Europe are good for technical tasks like working on websites and apps
- Look at the reviews for each candidate and only select the ones with 4* and over!
- Ask the candidates to register their available times, and make sure you interview them first. You can block out a morning/afternoon in your diary to do the interviews. 15 minutes each is good. Do them back-to-back, as some will be no shows :(
- No-shows and latecomers should not be considered. Pick at least two, and work with both before you decide
- I use an online scheduler to arrange interviews:

http://www.scheduleonce.com/. Set up a profile, and send candidates the link to book in. If they can't do that, then ...its bye bye

Where to get virtual assistants:
- PeoplePerHour.
- Fiverr   First order of $5 is free.
- www.onlinejobs.ph It's $49 a month to register, and you still have to pay for the VA.

CHAPTER FOURTEEN

THE DREADED F WORD IN BUSINESS... AND IN LIFE

"For the non-entrepreneur, no amount of credit availability will transform such person into a successful person, any more than buying me a piano would transform me into a successful musician."
~ *Muhota Wa Kimotho*[26]

Finance

I kept this to the end because although important, having a vision, passion and determination are as equally paramount and no amount of money will be enough for a business that does not have a plan. That phrase "Failing to

---

[26]   *From: http://www.creditkenya.com/2008/02/credt-not-only-way-out-of-poverty.html on 13th February 2016*

Plan is Planning to Fail" rings true especially for finance. This is definitely not the sexiest side of the business, possibly doesn't give you the wow factor that choosing a website layout or social media designs might give you, but your figures say a lot about how you run your business and will also determine how efficiently your business is being run.

Finance, without it life can be bleak and a business with no finance dies quickly...some can be resurrected but rarely, instead the business or the space it occupied is taken over quite quickly by another business that did keep its eye on its finances. Nearly 50% of new businesses fail within the first 5 years and one of the top reasons is insufficient capital[27] as well as poor planning –which are both linked to business finances.

Know your numbers

The key thing to note is that you must have a budget and a cash flow in place as the basics. They will both help you plan, anticipate and prevent any cash shortfall that you may have in the future. Most businesses fail because of a sudden cash shortage that they could have avoided if they had had a cash flow. The sooner you can anticipate a tight cash flow issue on the horizon the more time you have available to take action – for instance you could ask for an overdraft, extra time to pay a supplier, or find a way to sell more products.

Nowadays, there are many software packages and apps that can help you keep on top of your business finances. Most

---

[27] *Money you need to start up a business and pay for capital items and expenses in the first few months, before you make any sales*

banks have apps so you can check you finances at the touch of a button from your smartphone, there are also some software that are linked up to your bank account and can do your cash flow for you. For instance Mint in the US, and Money Dashboard in the UK are excellent for you to start monitoring your businesses finances and once you get bigger there are other packages like QuickBooks which are all cloud based and link up to your account. But obviously, the report from these software will only be as good as the information that you put into them. Do make sure that you keep invoices and receipts of all business purchases and expenses.

Budgets

Cash is the lifeblood of any business and the reason we go into business is to make a profit, so keeping your eyes on the money is key to having a successful business.

A budget is your plan expressed in monetary terms - so say you want to build a website, design logos, stationery, get policies and procedures in place and get an office etc. You need to have an idea of what each one would cost - phone around, search online and get quotes. Add up all these figures and this should give you an idea of how much it will cost you to start.

Then the flip side is to work out how much you expect to get – the income from the sale of your services and products. You'd have to identify the prices and quantities of your product/service that you are likely to sell, remember these are just estimates, unless you're lucky enough to have contracts in place when you first start out.

One challenge that you'd have, as a new business owner, is pricing your products properly - you're more likely to under price your products rather than over price and that comes from probably not having enough confidence to charge what your product or service is worth especially if it's a service. But you can charge more - but add value, 30-day money back guarantee, bonuses and extras may justify a higher price than your competitors.

Cash flow

Once you have done the budget. The next thing you will need is a cash flow, this really is the movement of your cash as it comes in or out of your business and is based on your budget – the timing of money coming in and going out. You will need money to pay expenses such as rent, stationery, stock, insurance and tax and this may have to be paid before you get paid, so you need to know the timing of these expenses. And this is why you need a cash flow forecast which helps you anticipate how much is coming in and out of the business each month (or weekly if needed). Once you have a budget and cash flow in place make sure you look at the reports monthly to see if your predicted figures look any thing like your actual figures.

Say for example you forecast that sales would be £1000 a month and at the end of the third month you have only made £500, you will need to find out why there is a discrepancy – Were your figures too optimistic? How much marketing have you done? Are your prices too high? You might want to look at your competitors and see what they're doing? Ask your customers; they are your greatest source of information as a new business and can give you insights into your business processes and how you can improve them.

To help you with your budgeting and cash flow, I have free Excel templates on my website for you to download.

It will be wise to get advice from an accountant, if you are struggling with keeping on top of your finances, they can help you to save money in the long run, giving you peace of mind and letting you get on with your passion of running your business – what you do best!

CHAPTER FIFTEEN

ACCEPT THAT CHANGE IS CONSTANT

"The End is the beginning."
- Winston Churchill[28]

We all change

Let me free you from something that holds us back over and over again: the need to be seen as never changing, i.e. in policies, rules or ideologies. To quote Emerson[29], in his profound essay about changing our minds ~ *" "Foolish consistency is the hobgoblin of little minds."*

Life is a journey, not a destination. We are growing, and everyday we learn something new; we read, we meet people, we see different trends. Ten years ago the world was a very

---

28   *Sir Winston Leonard Spencer-Churchill, (1874 – 1965) was a British statesman and the Prime Minister of the United Kingdom from 1940 to 1945 and again from 1951 to 1955.*

29   *First published in 1841 as Essays. After Essays: Second Series was published in 1844, Emerson corrected this volume and republished it in 1847 as Essays: First Series.*

different place. If you're reading this on a Kindle, mobile phone or iPad, you'll understand what I'm talking about. You wouldn't have done that ten years ago. So why should you not be free to change your stance on what you believe? Why can't we contradict ourselves?

"The way to get started is to quit talking and begin doing."
– Walt Disney[30]

Be confident

We have to be strong enough to stand up to our changing beliefs. Emerson attests that the only truth and judgement that matters is our own, not that of others. Sometimes, because of our need to conform, we dismiss our own creativity. We all have flashes of creativity and inspiration, but often we quickly disregard them as being stupid or impossible until we see someone else coming up with the same thoughts and realise that we had a great idea. How many ideas do you have now that are really yours? It's quite frightening to realise that as we grow older most of our thoughts are picked up from others; we're actually too scared to be different and to stand out as so.

We have enough within us to create what we need to survive. We just need to be bold enough to believe in ourselves.

---

[30]   *Walter Elias "Walt" Disney (1901 – 1966) was an American entrepreneur, animator, voice actor and film producer.*

When we hear speakers who tell us about their real experiences – their failure and success minus the gloss, it inspires us to take risks, too.

We are all unique and have our own abilities, talents or gifts to contribute before we leave. Are you going to do that? Are you going to bless us with your very own unique talents, skills and knowledge? Or are you going to take them back with you?

Rejection in business is common, and if you haven't failed many times then you haven't tried enough times.

It's often said that we use less than 10% of our brains. That's obviously a misquote because we use different parts of our brains for different reasons. However, what is true is that we don't use our full capacity. It's almost as if there is an invisible elastic band that keeps us reined in each time we reach out. We seem to go so far towards our goal - asking for some help, looking for a job, or whatever it is we want - and then run back to our comfort zone, possibly after asking only once or twice.

We forget that the most successful people in life, the ones we know of and read about, tried many times over - some thousands of times. We all know the story of the light bulb creator, Edison; he tried over 10,000 times. Our modern-day

Edison, Mr Dyson, tried over 5,000 times before his hoover worked, and Walt Disney went bankrupt three times before he built Disneyland.

Don't worry about getting your product perfect the first time, just start creating them, they will get better with time and with feedback from your customers. Consider this quote by by Reid Hoffman, the founder of LinkedIn:

> ## "If you are not embarrassed by the first version of your product, you've launched too late."

This should encourage you to produce new products and services as soon as possible, and concentrate on improvements after they have been launched, using feedback rather than wasting time trying to perfect it before the launch. Remember perfection is the enemy of progress.

MOJO Hacks:

- So, how many times are you willing to fail?
- Who is the one person you would like to meet that could take your business to the next level?
- Who are the people you need to meet in order to grow your business? Make a list of ten of them, and find ways to meet them or other people who can introduce you to them

If after reading all that you're probably wondering "Where do I start from?" Just start from where you are. You can also go to my website www.unleashyourbusinessmojo.com for additional resources and tips to guide you through your journey into self-employment.

The one way to fail is to not keep up with your business in the early months. I suggest you work on it every week for at least six months before you call time on it - and even then it would be too early. Forget about overnight success - that is very rare. And what is considered overnight success is actually someone working away behind the scenes and then suddenly what they're doing goes viral. If you want to go viral, keep working. Change tack, but don't give up.

As you go forth and build your legacy I leave you with this quote from Edmund Burke[31], which reminds us all that we are only human and that we all need reassurance, sometimes.

> *"Applaud us when we run*
> *Console us when we fall*
> *But cheer us when we recover."*

---

[31]   *Edmund Burke (1729 - 1797) was an Irish statesman born in Dublin, as well as an author, orator, political theorist, and philosopher..*